WHEN FORMER U.S. AIR FORCE PILOT **CAROL DANVERS**
WAS CAUGHT IN THE EXPLOSION OF AN ALIEN DEVICE,
SHE WAS IMBUED WITH SUPERHUMAN POWERS. AS AN
AVENGER SHE USED HER GIFTS TO PROTECT THE PLANET.
NOW A NEW CHAPTER AWAITS, YET SHE IS AND
ALWAYS WILL BE EARTH'S MIGHTIEST HERO. SHE IS..

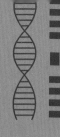

CAPTAIN MARVEL

RISE OF ALPHA FLIGHT

MICHELE FAZEKAS
& TARA BUTTERS
WRITERS

KRIS ANKA (#1-5)
& FELIPE SMITH (#3-5)

MATTHEW
WILSON
COLOR ARTIST

VC'S JOE CARAMAGNA
LETTERER

SANA AMANAT
EDITOR

JENNIFER GRÜNWALD
COLLECTION EDITOR

SARAH BRUNSTAD
ASSOCIATE EDITOR

ALEX STARBUCK
ASSOCIATE MANAGING EDITOR

MARK D. BEAZLEY
EDITOR, SPECIAL PROJECTS

JEFF YOUNGQUIST
VP, PRODUCTION & SPECIAL PROJECTS

DAVID GABRIEL
SVP PRINT, SALES & MARKETING

JAY BOWEN
BOOK DESIGNER

AXEL ALONSO
EDITOR IN CHIEF

JOE QUESADA
CHIEF CREATIVE OFFICER

DAN BUCKLEY
PUBLISHER

ALAN FINE
EXECUTIVE PRODUCER

CAPTAIN MARVEL VOL. 1: RISE OF ALPHA FLIGHT. Contains material originally published in magazine form as CAPTAIN MARVEL #1-5. First printing 2016. ISBN# 978-0-7851-9642-6. Published by MARVEL WORLDWIDE, INC., a subsidiary of MARVEL ENTERTAINMENT, LLC. OFFICE OF PUBLICATION: 135 West 50th Street, New York, NY 10020. Copyright © 2016 MARVEL No similarity between any of the names, characters, persons, and/or institutions in this magazine with those of any living or dead person or institution is intended, and any such similarity which may exist is purely coincidental. **Printed in Canada.** ALAN FINE, President, Marvel Entertainment; DAN BUCKLEY, President, TV, Publishing & Brand Management; JOE QUESADA, Chief Creative Officer; TOM BREVOORT, SVP of Publishing; DAVID BOGART, SVP of Business Affairs & Operations, Publishing & Partnership; C.B. CEBULSKI, VP of Brand Management & Development, Asia; DAVID GABRIEL, SVP of Sales & Marketing, Publishing; JEFF YOUNGQUIST, VP of Production & Special Projects; DAN CARR, Executive Director of Publishing Technology; ALEX MORALES, Director of Publishing Operations; SUSAN CRESPI, Production Manager; STAN LEE, Chairman Emeritus. For information regarding advertising in Marvel Comics or on Marvel.com, please contact Vit DeBellis, Integrated Sales Manager, at vdebellis@marvel.com. For Marvel subscription inquiries, please call 888-511-5480. **Manufactured between 5/27/2016 and 7/4/2016 by SOLISCO PRINTERS, SCOTT, QC, CANADA.**

10 9 8 7 6 5 4 3 2 1

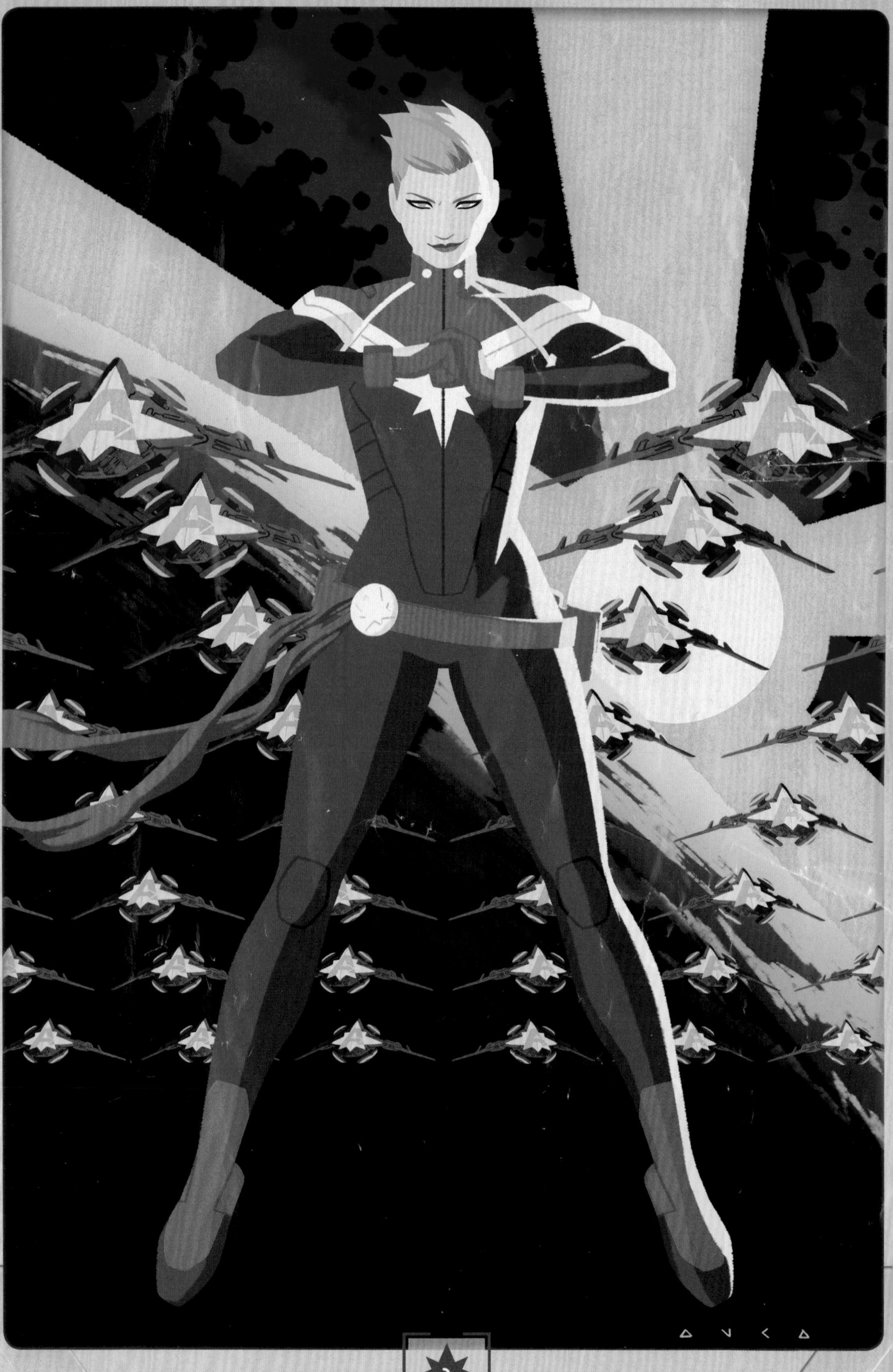

WOO-HOO! LIKE BULLS-EYEING WOMP RATS IN A... WAIT, WHAT'S THE LINE?

Eugene Judd, "PUCK"

PUCK, YOUR THREE O'CLOCK, WATCH IT.

ALL RIGHT, K! GREAT SHOT!

CUT THE CHITCHAT AND PAY ATTENTION, WILL YOU?

Jeanne-Marie Beaubier, "AURORA"

I WILL DO THAT. FOR YOU, AURORA

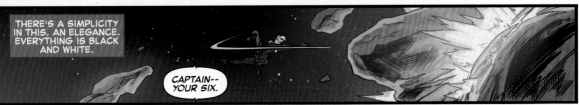

THERE'S A SIMPLICITY IN THIS. AN ELEGANCE. EVERYTHING IS BLACK AND WHITE.

CAPTAIN-- YOUR SIX.

BUZZ BUZZ BUZZ BUZZ

THE VECTORS ARE GETTING HARDER TO PREDICT. THEY'RE RICOCHETING.

Walter Langkowski, "SASQUATCH"

EVERYBODY PULL IT BACK A LITTLE.

AND EVEN WHEN YOU'RE GETTING CLOBBERED, AT LEAST YOU KNOW WHERE YOU STAND.

DANVERS, THREE O'CLOCK!

GRAY AREAS ARE NOT MY THING. I PREFER BLACK AND WHITE.

USUALLY.

CAPTAIN, GET OUT OF THERE! CAPTAIN!

STILL...THIS MIGHT'VE BEEN A REALLY BAD IDEA.

DON'T TELL ME THAT'S ALL YOU'RE BRINGING.

GOOD NEWS ABOUT THE NEW HAIRCUT, *RHODEY*-- I'M SUPER LOW-MAINTENANCE NOW.

I WANT YOU TO TAKE A LOOK AT MY HAIRSTYLE, BECAUSE IF I WAS DEPLOYING FOR TWO YEARS I'D SURE AS HELL BRING MORE THAN A BACKPACK.

I'LL DO LAUNDRY.

Lt. James Rhodes, "WAR MACHINE"

GOTTA BE HONEST, I'M SURPRISED YOU TOOK THIS GIG.

DIDN'T REALLY THINK I COULD TURN IT DOWN.

I WOULD'VE.

OH, HONEY, YOU ARE TERRIBLE AT PEP TALKS.

I'M JUST SAYING I'VE GOT ENOUGH HEADACHES ON *THIS* PLANET. I DON'T NEED TO LEAVE THE ATMOSPHERE FOR MORE.

YOU'VE BEEN A MEMBER OF A TEAM. BUT NOW YOU'RE GONNA BE *THE COACH*. IT'S DIFFERENT.

GOOD. *DIFFERENT* IS WHAT I WANT.

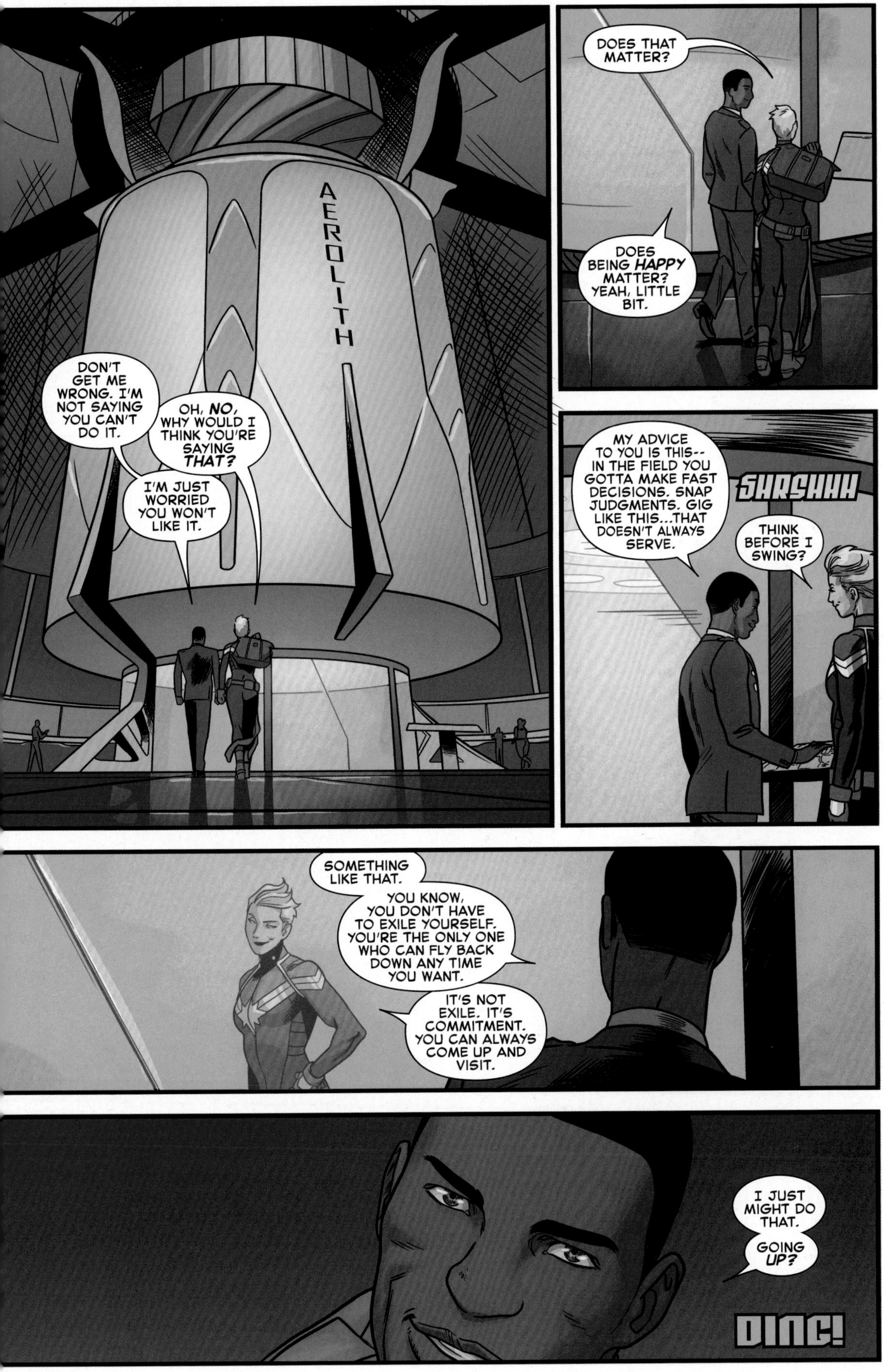
AEROLITH
DON'T GET ME WRONG. I'M NOT SAYING YOU CAN'T DO IT.
OH, NO, WHY WOULD I THINK YOU'RE SAYING THAT?
I'M JUST WORRIED YOU WON'T LIKE IT.
DOES THAT MATTER?
DOES BEING HAPPY MATTER? YEAH, LITTLE BIT.
MY ADVICE TO YOU IS THIS-- IN THE FIELD YOU GOTTA MAKE FAST DECISIONS. SNAP JUDGMENTS. GIG LIKE THIS...THAT DOESN'T ALWAYS SERVE.
SHRSHHH
THINK BEFORE I SWING?
SOMETHING LIKE THAT.
YOU KNOW, YOU DON'T HAVE TO EXILE YOURSELF. YOU'RE THE ONLY ONE WHO CAN FLY BACK DOWN ANY TIME YOU WANT.
IT'S NOT EXILE. IT'S COMMITMENT. YOU CAN ALWAYS COME UP AND VISIT.
I JUST MIGHT DO THAT.
GOING UP?
DING!

HE'S WORRIED I WON'T LIKE IT.

SHRAMM

AW, RHODEY LOVES ME.

TWO YEARS ON A SPACE STATION IN GEOSTATIONARY ORBIT, 250 KILOMETERS ABOVE THE EARTH'S SURFACE.

WHAT'S NOT TO LIKE?

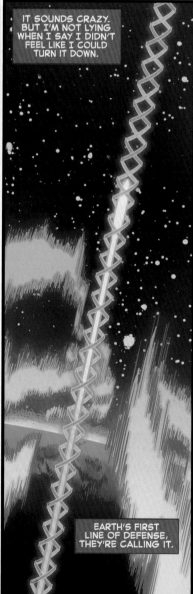

IT SOUNDS CRAZY. BUT I'M NOT LYING WHEN I SAY I DIDN'T FEEL LIKE I COULD TURN IT DOWN.

EARTH'S FIRST LINE OF DEFENSE, THEY'RE CALLING IT.

I LIKE BEING ON A TEAM. BUT MORE THAN THAT, I LIKE A MISSION. A PURPOSE.

AND THE BEST WAY TO FIGHT THREATS AGAINST THE GALAXY...

...IS MAKING SURE THEY NEVER GET THERE.
BESIDES I'M NOT ONE TO SIT STILL FOR LONG...NOT WHEN YOU CAN GET A VIEW LIKE THIS.
A.F.S.S.
Alpha Flight
Space Station

A COUPLE OF YEARS OUT OF THE SPOTLIGHT ISN'T A BAD THING. IT'LL BE NICE TO BE NORMAL FOR A WHILE.

OR AT LEAST...*MY* VERSION OF NORMAL.

DING

EUGENE JUDD. PEOPLE CALL ME--

PUCK. GLAD TO WORK WITH YOU. QUITE THE WELCOME COMMITTEE.

EVERYBODY'S JUST EXCITED TO MEET YOU. COME ON--I'LL GIVE YOU THE TOUR.

THAT'LL HAVE TO WAIT.

OUR CELEBRITY IS LATE FOR A MEETING WITH THE *ERIDANI* DELEGATION.

COMMANDER DANVERS, WELCOME TO THE ALPHA FLIGHT SPACE STATION.

ABIGA
BRAN
Alpha Flig
Lt. Command

DANVERS! WHAT'S SHAKIN'?

FIRST DAY ON THE JOB.

AH. SORRY. HATE FIRST DAYS. LITTLE HELP?

GUARDIANS AND ME ARE ON A PITSTOP BEFORE WE DEPLOY. JUST NEEDED SOME SUPPLIES.

SO YOU'RE STEALING A BUNCH OF STUFF.

NO. NO--WELL, YEAH.

YOU KNOW I LIKE YOU, ROCKET, BUT AS COMMANDER OF THIS STATION, I FEEL LIKE I CAN'T LET YOU STEAL A NUKE.

COMMANDER? OF THE WHOLE SHEBANG? NO KIDDING. WEIRD.

WHAT'S SO WEIRD?

JUST SURPRISED IS ALL. CAPTAIN MARVEL TAKES A DESK JOB. AREN'T YOU GONNA BE BORED?

IT'S NOT A DESK JOB.

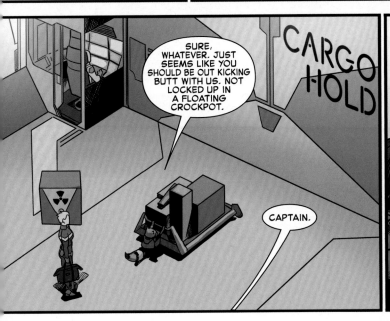

SURE, WHATEVER. JUST SEEMS LIKE YOU SHOULD BE OUT KICKING BUTT WITH US. NOT LOCKED UP IN A FLOATING CROCKPOT.

CARGO HOLD

CAPTAIN.

THE DELEGATION IS WAITING IN THE CONFERENCE ROOM.

...

DESK JOB.

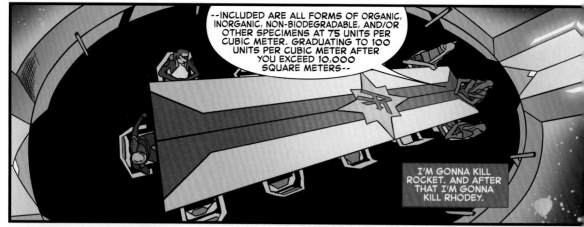

--INCLUDED ARE ALL FORMS OF ORGANIC, INORGANIC, NON-BIODEGRADABLE, AND/OR OTHER SPECIMENS AT 75 UNITS PER CUBIC METER. GRADUATING TO 100 UNITS PER CUBIC METER AFTER YOU EXCEED 10,000 SQUARE METERS--

I'M GONNA KILL ROCKET. AND AFTER THAT I'M GONNA KILL RHODEY.

--IN THE EVENT THAT RADIATION LEVELS OF INDUSTRIAL WASTE EXCEED 50 MICROSIEVERTS--

THE GREAT CAPTAIN MARVEL, TALKING ABOUT GARBAGE.

ARE WE BORING YOU, CAPTAIN MARVEL?

OR WOULD YOU PREFER THE ALPHA FLIGHT SPACE STATION BE AS POLLUTED AS THAT PLANET YOU CALL HOME?

EXCUSE ME?

THE CAPTAIN'S ONLY JUST ARRIVED AND IS ACCLIMATING TO HER NEW POSITION. PLEASE DON'T BE OFFENDED BY HER BEHAVIOR.

YOU KNOW WHAT'S OFFENSIVE? GETTING GOUGED ON SERVICES THAT HAD BEEN PRE-NEGOTIATED A YEAR AGO. NICE TO SEE THE TRASH BUSINESS IN SPACE IS MOBBED UP, TOO--

DANVERS!

HOW DARE YOU SUGGEST--

SEE? I WAS LISTENING.

COMMANDER. SENSORS HAVE DETECTED A MASSIVE ASTEROID COLLISION--DEBRIS WILL BE IN RANGE IN LESS THAN TWENTY MINUTES.

ENSIGN, YOUR TIMING IS IMPECCABLE.

CAPTAIN, THE ALPHA FLIGHT CAN HANDLE IT, YOU ARE NEEDED HERE--

YOU CAN HANDLE THIS, BRAND. BESIDES HE LIKES YOU BETTER.

ALPHA FLIGHT... ASSEMBLE.

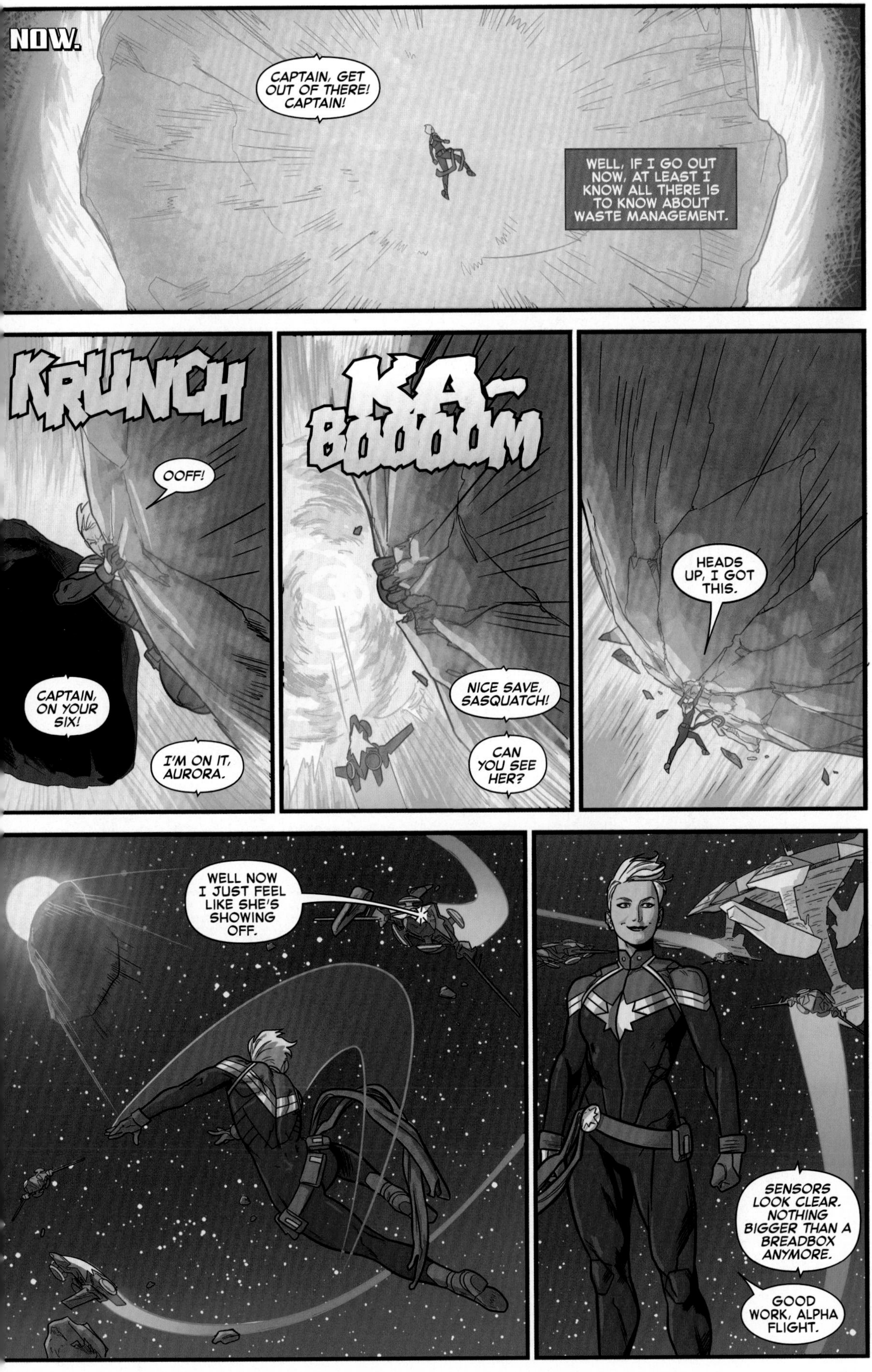
NOW.
CAPTAIN, GET OUT OF THERE! CAPTAIN!
WELL, IF I GO OUT NOW, AT LEAST I KNOW ALL THERE IS TO KNOW ABOUT WASTE MANAGEMENT.
KRUNCH
OOFF!
CAPTAIN, ON YOUR SIX!
I'M ON IT, AURORA.
KA-BOOOOM
NICE SAVE, SASQUATCH!
CAN YOU SEE HER?
HEADS UP, I GOT THIS.
WELL NOW I JUST FEEL LIKE SHE'S SHOWING OFF.
SENSORS LOOK CLEAR. NOTHING BIGGER THAN A BREADBOX ANYMORE.
GOOD WORK, ALPHA FLIGHT.

THAT WAS A NICE SHOT, WALT. SAVED MY TAIL.

COULDN'T LET YOU DO ALL THE WORK.

YOU SHOULD CHECK OUT THE SHOWERS, CAP. THE RAIN FEATURE IS DELIGHTFUL.

I WILL. I'VE GOT METEOR DUST IN EVERY CREVICE.

WELL, LET ME KNOW IF YOU NEED HELP WITH THAT.

VERY KIND OF YOU, EUGENE.

YOU'RE A CRETIN.

WILL YOU BE JOINING US ON EVERY MISSION, CAPTAIN? I THOUGHT YOU'D BE MORE COMMAND THAN OUT IN THE FIELD.

I HAVE NO INTENTION OF SITTING BEHIND A DESK FOR TWO YEARS.

AND GUYS. CALL ME CAROL.

CAPTAIN MARVEL?

SORRY TO INTRUDE... I'VE BEEN LOOKING INTO THE ASTEROID COLLISION AND FOUND SOME TROUBLING READINGS.

DEFINE TROUBLING.

Lieutenant Wendy Kawasaki SCIENCE OFFICER

THERE WAS NO COLLISION.

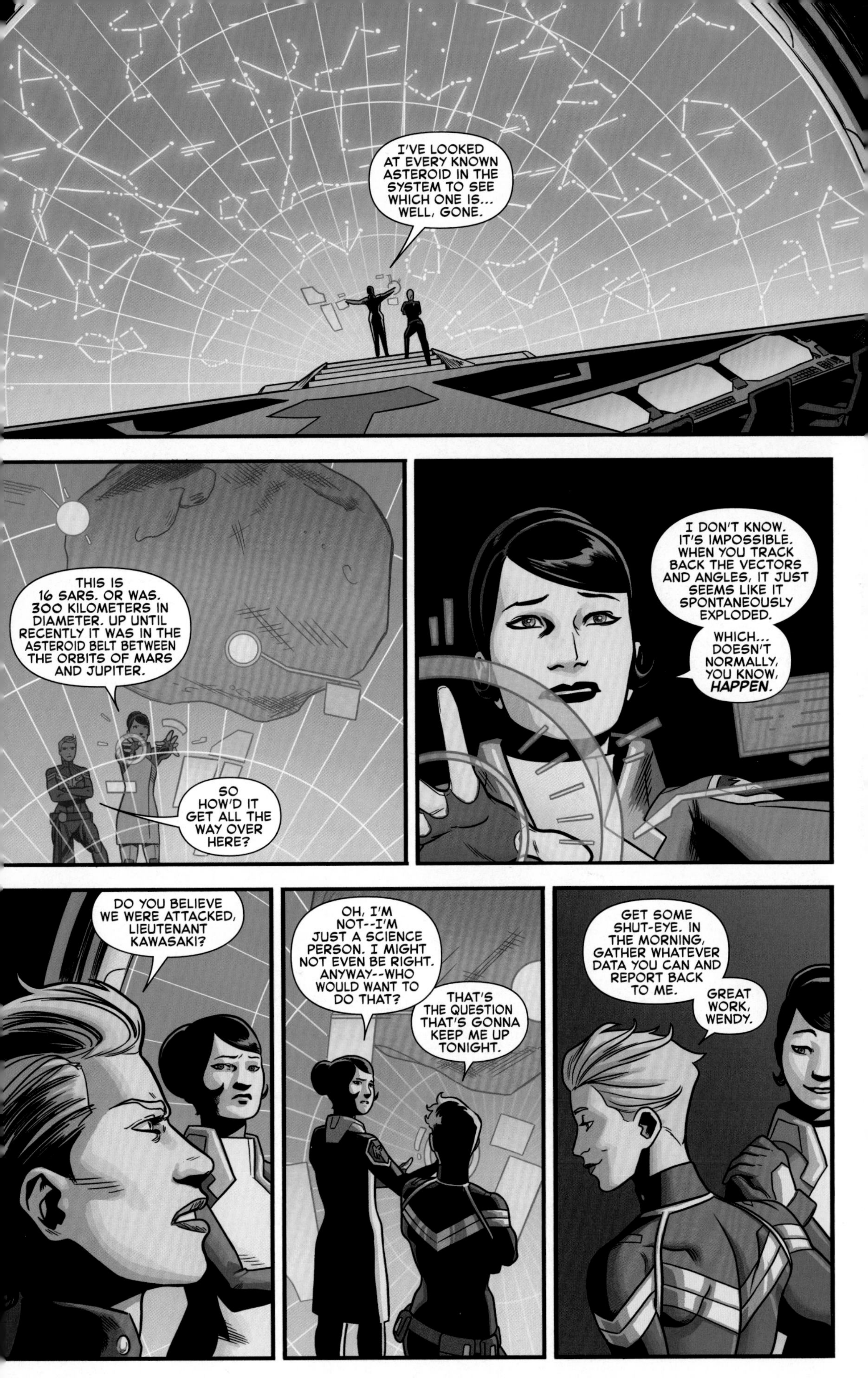
I'VE LOOKED AT EVERY KNOWN ASTEROID IN THE SYSTEM TO SEE WHICH ONE IS... WELL, GONE.
THIS IS 16 SARS. OR WAS. 300 KILOMETERS IN DIAMETER. UP UNTIL RECENTLY IT WAS IN THE ASTEROID BELT BETWEEN THE ORBITS OF MARS AND JUPITER.
SO HOW'D IT GET ALL THE WAY OVER HERE?
I DON'T KNOW. IT'S IMPOSSIBLE. WHEN YOU TRACK BACK THE VECTORS AND ANGLES, IT JUST SEEMS LIKE IT SPONTANEOUSLY EXPLODED.
WHICH... DOESN'T NORMALLY, YOU KNOW, *HAPPEN*.
DO YOU BELIEVE WE WERE ATTACKED, LIEUTENANT KAWASAKI?
OH, I'M NOT--I'M JUST A SCIENCE PERSON. I MIGHT NOT EVEN BE RIGHT. ANYWAY--WHO WOULD WANT TO DO THAT?
THAT'S THE QUESTION THAT'S GONNA KEEP ME UP TONIGHT.
GET SOME SHUT-EYE. IN THE MORNING, GATHER WHATEVER DATA YOU CAN AND REPORT BACK TO ME.
GREAT WORK, WENDY.

CAPTAIN MARVEL'S QUARTERS. 0200 Hours.

AAAND I'M NOT SLEEPING. I JINXED MYSELF.

WOULD'VE THOUGHT TWELVE ROUNDS WITH AN ASTEROID FIELD WOULD'VE TUCKERED YOU OUT, DANVERS.

FEELING LIKE A SITTING DUCK KEEPS ME AWAKE. CAN'T SLEEP EITHER?

CLANK CLANK CLUNK

DON'T SLEEP, USUALLY. SIDE EFFECT OF BEING BITE-SIZED. EVERYTHING HURTS.

THAT'S AWFUL. I'M SORRY.

JUST THE WAY IT IS. BONUS OF NOT SLEEPING IS I GET TO TAKE UP NEW HOBBIES. I'LL KNIT THE HELL OUT OF A SCARF FOR YOU.

MAKE IT A RED ONE.

SORRY YOU TOOK THIS GIG YET?

TAKES MORE THAN SOMEBODY THROWING ROCKS TO SCARE ME OFF. THOUGH BRAND WOULD BE HAPPY TO SEE ME GO.

WHAT MAKES YOU SAY THAT?

BARELY CONCEALED HOSTILITY ISN'T USUALLY LOST ON ME.

BRAND DOESN'T DO SOCIAL INTERACTIONS REAL WELL. BUT SHE'S SQUARED AWAY. SAVED MY BACON MORE THAN ONCE.

I DON'T DOUBT IT. BUT IT'S PRETTY OBVIOUS SHE WANTED THIS JOB. AND THEY GAVE IT TO ME.

ACTUALLY... SHE TURNED IT DOWN.

CHRP

CAPTAIN MARVEL-- I FOUND SOMETHING.

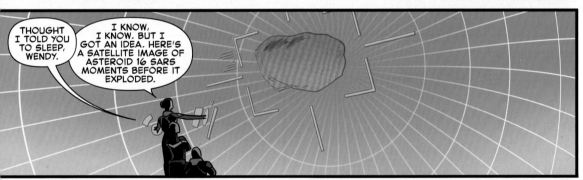

THOUGHT I TOLD YOU TO SLEEP, WENDY.

I KNOW, I KNOW. BUT I GOT AN IDEA. HERE'S A SATELLITE IMAGE OF ASTEROID 16 SARS MOMENTS BEFORE IT EXPLODED.

HERE IT IS MAGNIFIED FIFTY TIMES. SEE THAT WHITE DOT?

IT'S AN ALIEN SHIP.

HOW CAN YOU TELL?

BECAUSE IT HAS AN ENERGY SIGNATURE. AND IT MATCHES ONE KNOWN ALIEN SPECIES IN OUR DATABASE.

SENSORS PICKED UP AN ALIEN VESSEL ON DIRECT APPROACH.

IS IT AN ERIDANI SHIP?

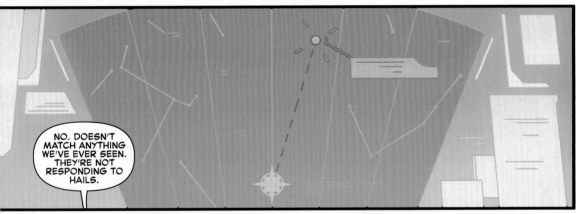

NO. DOESN'T MATCH ANYTHING WE'VE EVER SEEN. THEY'RE NOT RESPONDING TO HAILS.

HOW LONG BEFORE IT REACHES US?

THIRTY MINUTES UNTIL FIRING RANGE.

WAKE UP, ALPHA FLIGHT.

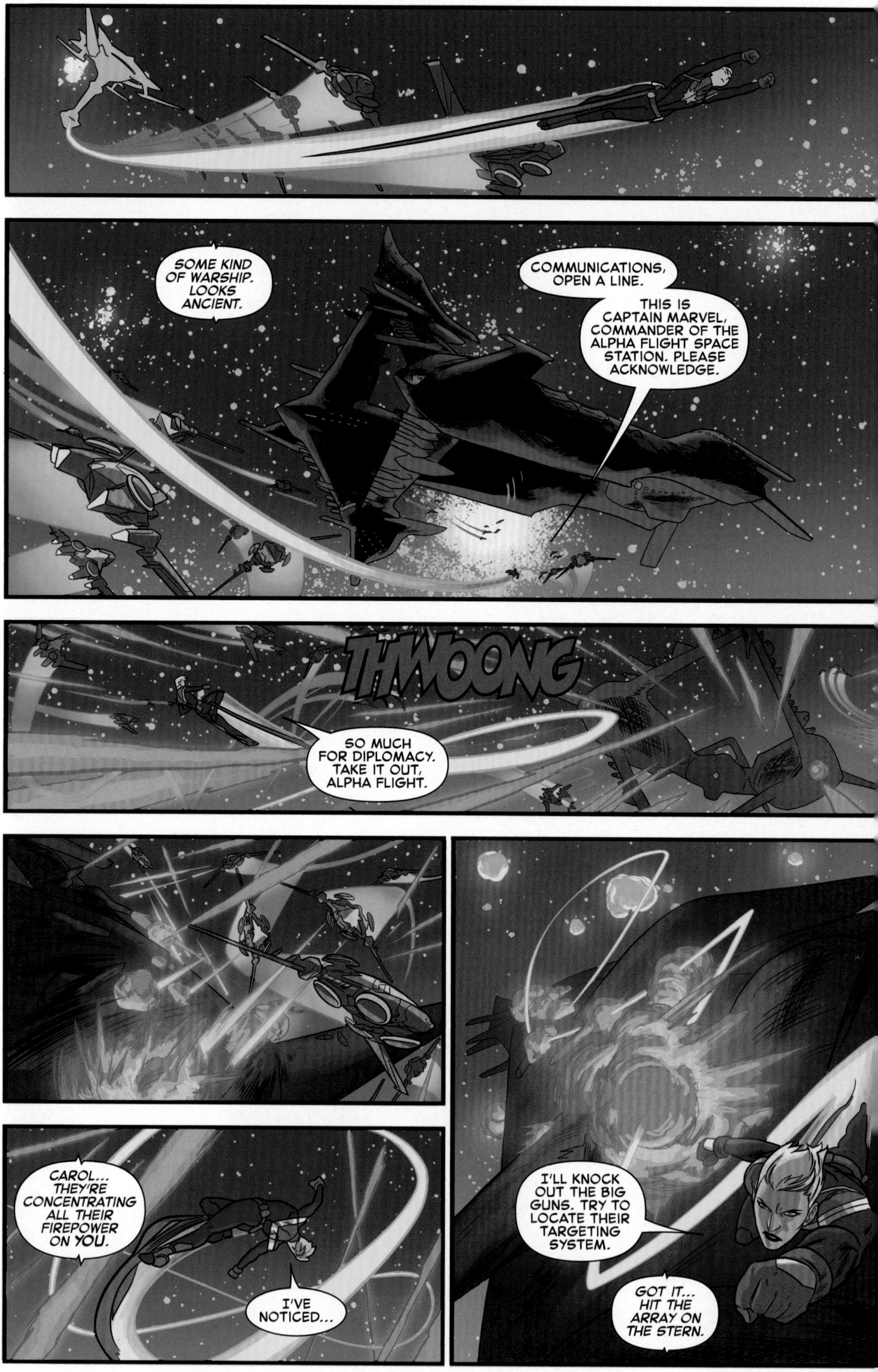
SOME KIND OF WARSHIP. LOOKS ANCIENT.
COMMUNICATIONS, OPEN A LINE.
THIS IS CAPTAIN MARVEL, COMMANDER OF THE ALPHA FLIGHT SPACE STATION. PLEASE ACKNOWLEDGE.
THWOONG
SO MUCH FOR DIPLOMACY. TAKE IT OUT, ALPHA FLIGHT.
CAROL... THEY'RE CONCENTRATING ALL THEIR FIREPOWER ON YOU.
I'VE NOTICED...
I'LL KNOCK OUT THE BIG GUNS. TRY TO LOCATE THEIR TARGETING SYSTEM.
GOT IT... HIT THE ARRAY ON THE STERN.

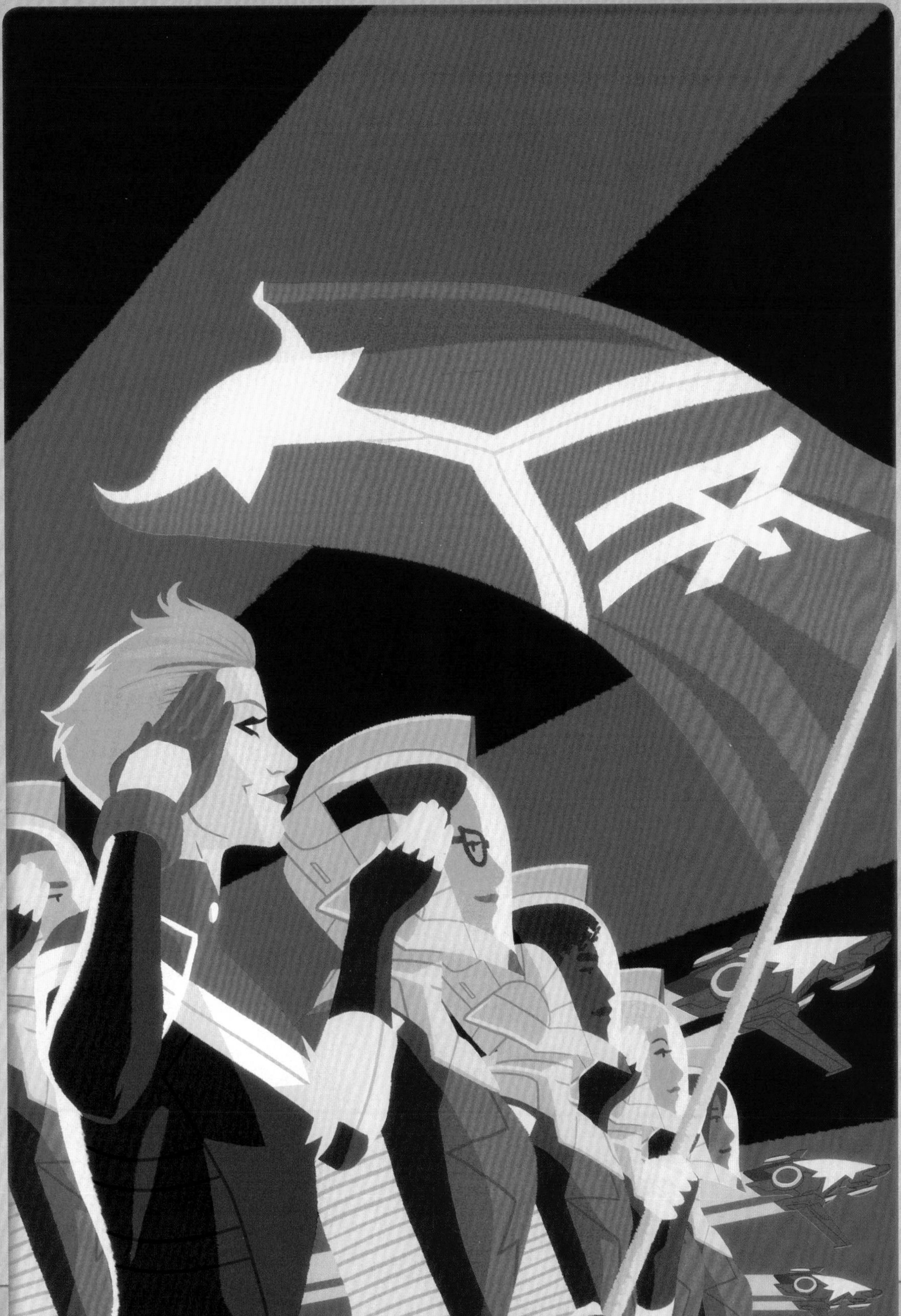

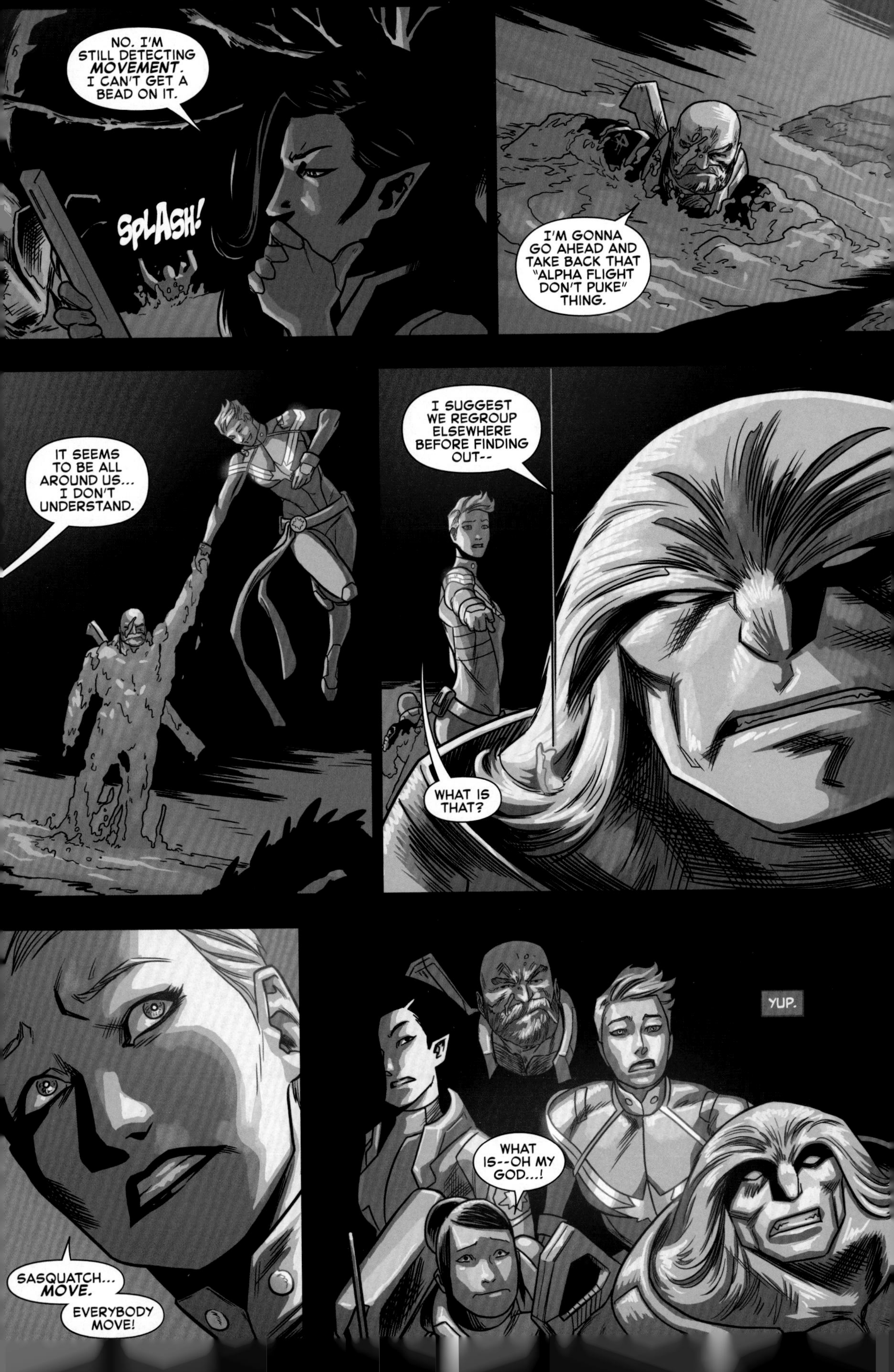
NO. I'M STILL DETECTING MOVEMENT. I CAN'T GET A BEAD ON IT.
SPLASH!
I'M GONNA GO AHEAD AND TAKE BACK THAT "ALPHA FLIGHT DON'T PUKE" THING.
IT SEEMS TO BE ALL AROUND US... I DON'T UNDERSTAND.
I SUGGEST WE REGROUP ELSEWHERE BEFORE FINDING OUT--
WHAT IS THAT?
SASQUATCH... MOVE.
EVERYBODY MOVE!
WHAT IS--OH MY GOD...!
YUP.

UH, COMMANDER BRAND...DID YOU HEAR ME?

YEP. BUT TELL ME AGAIN JUST TO BE SURE.

THE ERIDANI DELEGATION IS DEMANDING TO BE RELEASED. AND TO BE APPOINTED COUNSEL.

AND... THEY DON'T LIKE OUR FOOD.

THIS SHOWS UP ON *OUR* DOORSTEP. ON A STATION IN THE SHAPE OF A HALA STAR. UNDER THE COMMAND OF A WOMAN WITH A HALA STAR ON HER CHEST.

DON'T TELL ME THAT'S A COINCIDENCE.

THE ERIDANI AMBASSADOR IS DEMANDING A MEETING. THEY'RE CONVENING AN EMERGENCY SESSION OF THE INTERGALACTIC COUNCIL. AND THE PRESIDENT CALLED.

TWICE.

TAKE A MESSAGE.

WITH CAPTAIN MARVEL ON A MISSION, THEY'RE ALL DEMANDING TO TALK TO *YOU,* COMMANDER. WE CAN'T HOLD THEM OFF FOREVER.

I SUPPOSE YOU'RE RIGHT, ENSIGN.

CONGRATULATIONS. YOU'VE BEEN APPOINTED ACTING COUNSEL TO THE ERIDANI. LET'S SEE IF THEY CAN GIVE US SOME ANSWERS.

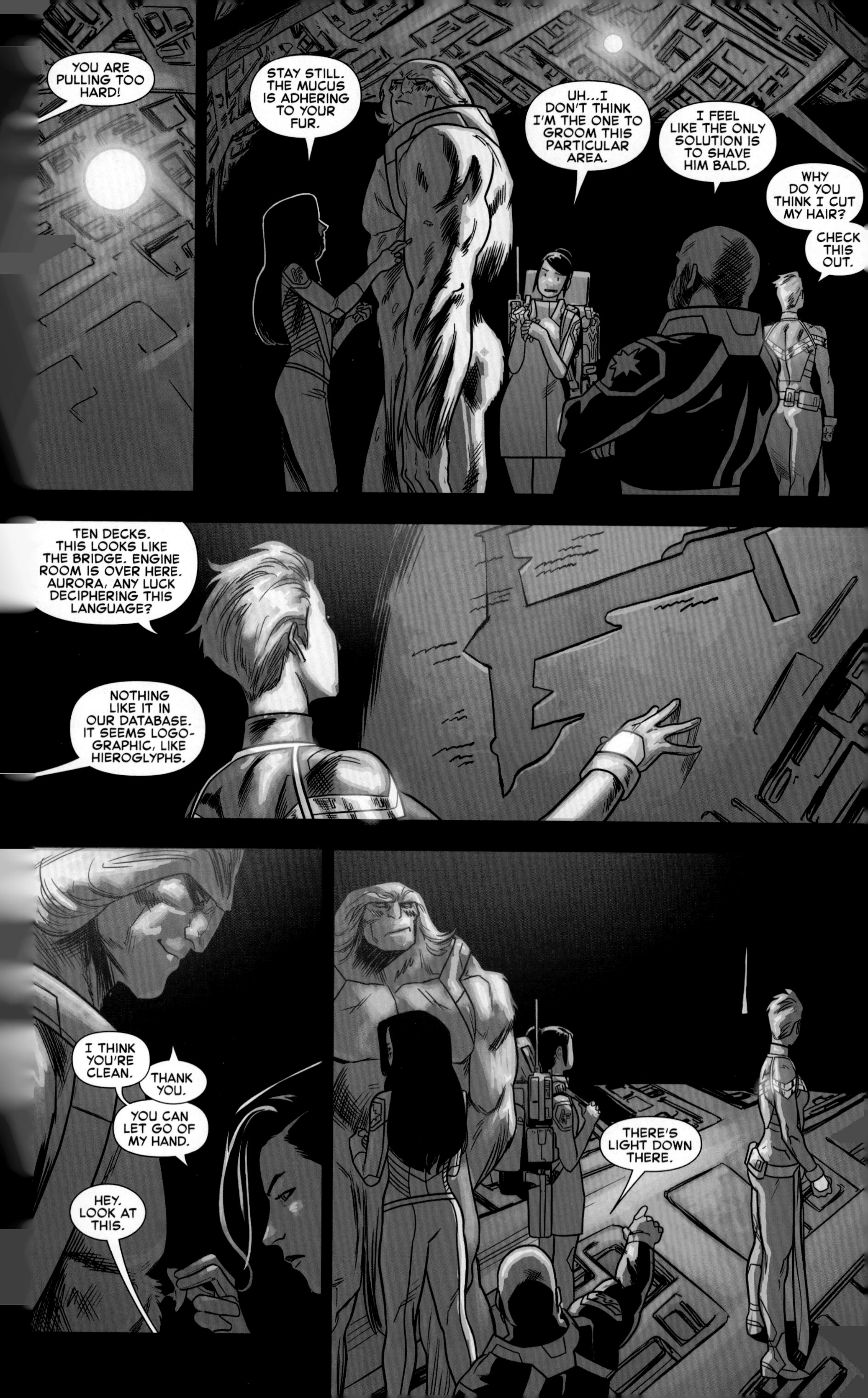
YOU ARE PULLING TOO HARD!
STAY STILL. THE MUCUS IS ADHERING TO YOUR FUR.
UH...I DON'T THINK I'M THE ONE TO GROOM THIS PARTICULAR AREA.
I FEEL LIKE THE ONLY SOLUTION IS TO SHAVE HIM BALD.
WHY DO YOU THINK I CUT MY HAIR?
CHECK THIS OUT.
TEN DECKS. THIS LOOKS LIKE THE BRIDGE. ENGINE ROOM IS OVER HERE. AURORA, ANY LUCK DECIPHERING THIS LANGUAGE?
NOTHING LIKE IT IN OUR DATABASE. IT SEEMS LOGO-GRAPHIC, LIKE HIEROGLYPHS.
I THINK YOU'RE CLEAN.
THANK YOU.
YOU CAN LET GO OF MY HAND.
HEY. LOOK AT THIS.
THERE'S LIGHT DOWN THERE.

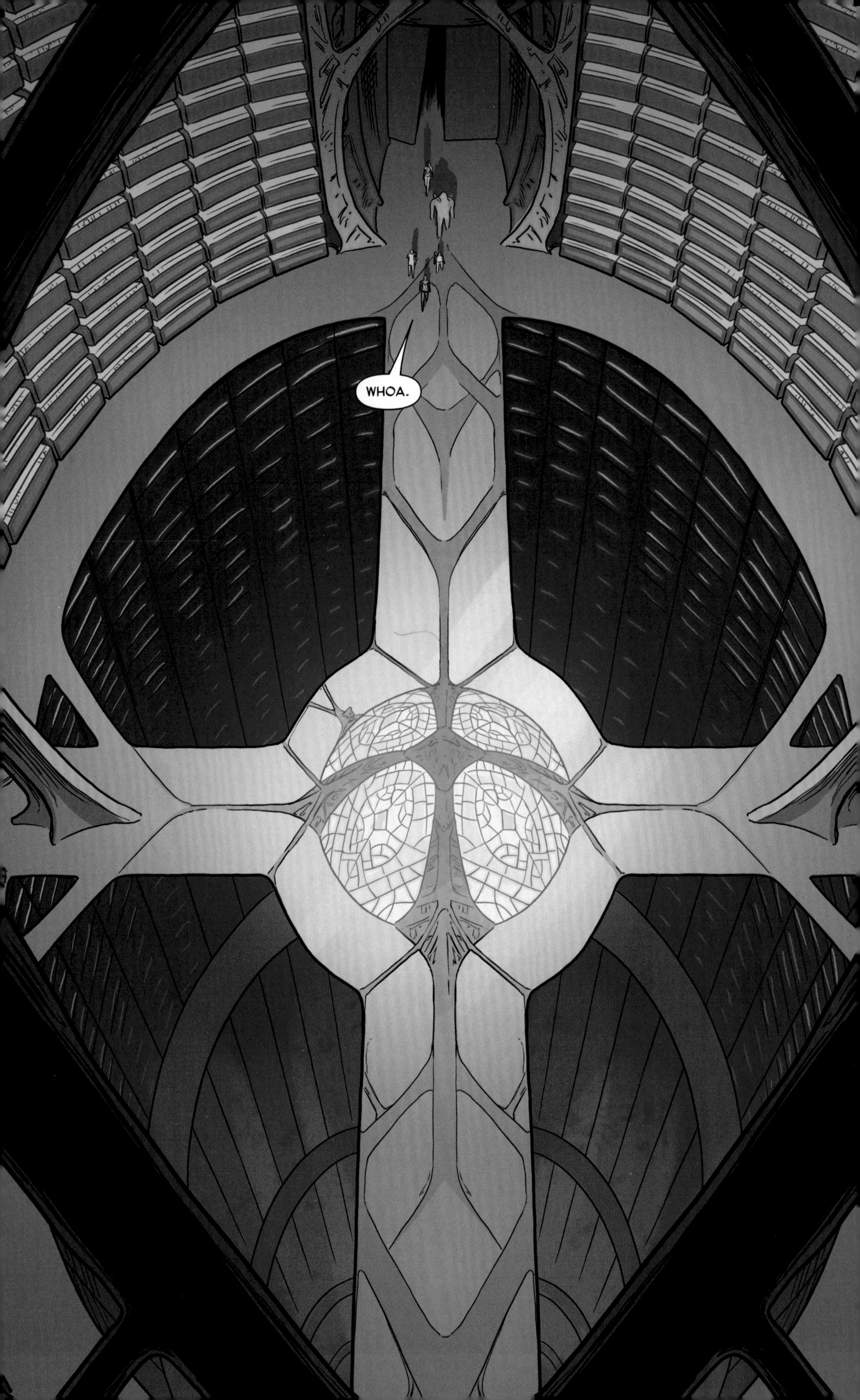
WHOA.

YOU HAVE NO STANDING TO KEEP US IN CUSTODY! WE HAVE DIPLOMATIC IMMUNITY.

IMMUNITY DOESN'T EXTEND TO ATTACKING A SPACE STATION.

LT. COMMANDER BRAND, YOU SEEM TO BE A REASONABLE PERSON. SURELY YOU CAN SEE CAPTAIN MARVEL ACTED RASHLY.

SHE ACTED ON THE EVIDENCE. I WOULD'VE DONE THE SAME THING.

WHAT EVIDENCE? I DEMAND YOU SHOW US IMMEDIATELY.

I DON'T HAVE TO SHOW YOU ANYTHING.

ACTUALLY, PURSUANT TO ARTICLE XIV-B OF THE INTERGALACTIC TREATY OF AMITY AND COMMERCE, THEY HAVE THE RIGHT TO SEE ANY EVIDENCE AGAINST THEM. M-MA'AM.

THANK YOU, COUNSELOR.

THIS IS IMPOSSIBLE.

NO, IT'S AN ERIDANI SHIP BLOWING UP AN ASTEROID, WHICH IS ABSOLUTELY POSSIBLE.

YOU'RE A FOOL, COMMANDER.

THAT ENERGY SIGNATURE COMES FROM A SHORT-RANGE VESSEL. IT COULD NEVER REACH THAT DISTANCE FROM OUR HOME PLANET. WHICH MEANS IT LAUNCHED FROM EARTH...OR FROM THIS STATION.

YOUR ENEMY IS WITHIN. AND PLOTTING AGAINST YOU STILL.

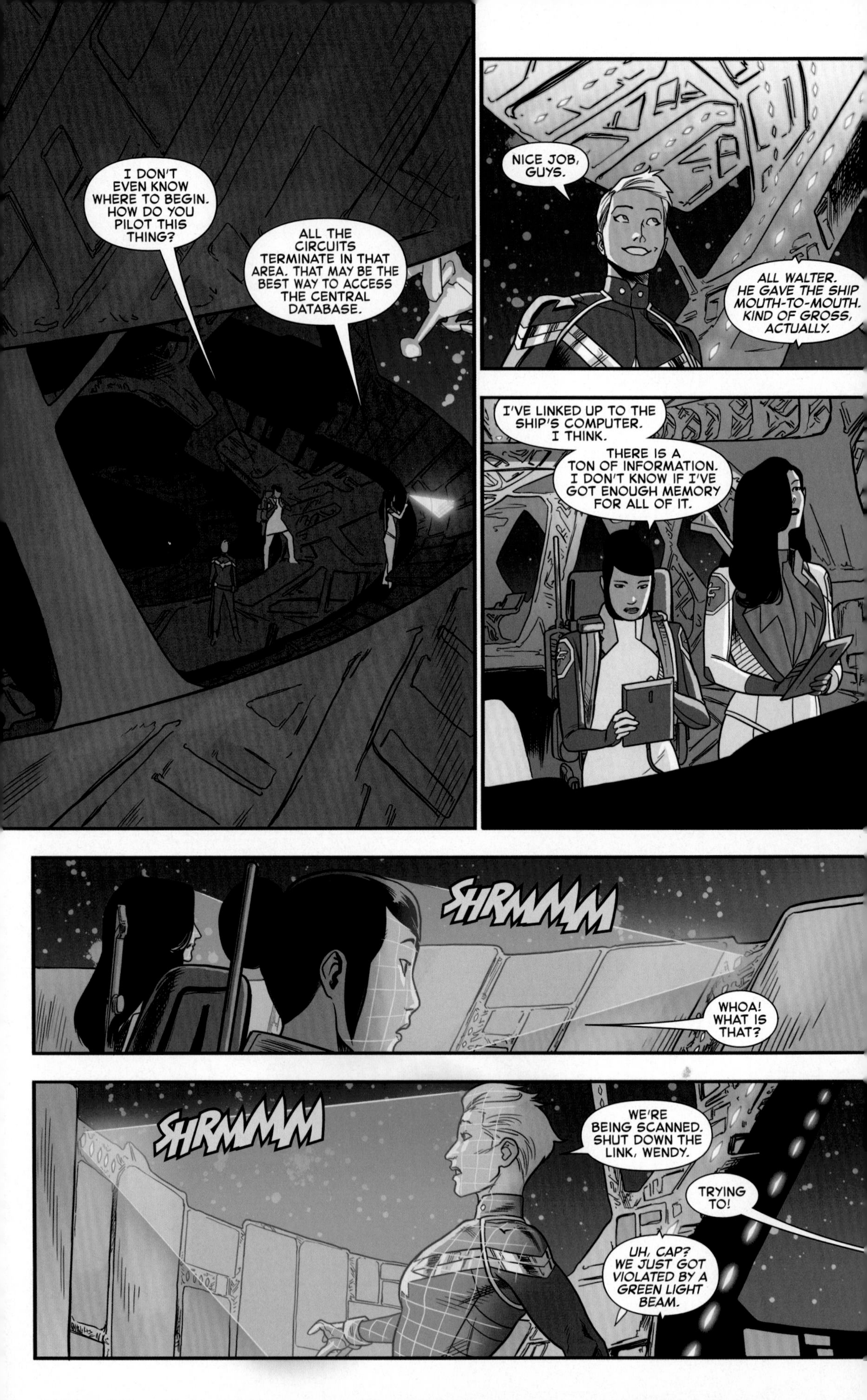
I DON'T EVEN KNOW WHERE TO BEGIN. HOW DO YOU PILOT THIS THING?
ALL THE CIRCUITS TERMINATE IN THAT AREA. THAT MAY BE THE BEST WAY TO ACCESS THE CENTRAL DATABASE.
NICE JOB, GUYS.
ALL WALTER. HE GAVE THE SHIP MOUTH-TO-MOUTH. KIND OF GROSS, ACTUALLY.
I'VE LINKED UP TO THE SHIP'S COMPUTER. I THINK.
THERE IS A TON OF INFORMATION. I DON'T KNOW IF I'VE GOT ENOUGH MEMORY FOR ALL OF IT.
SHRMMMM
WHOA! WHAT IS THAT?
SHRMMM
WE'RE BEING SCANNED. SHUT DOWN THE LINK, WENDY.
TRYING TO!
UH, CAP? WE JUST GOT VIOLATED BY A GREEN LIGHT BEAM.

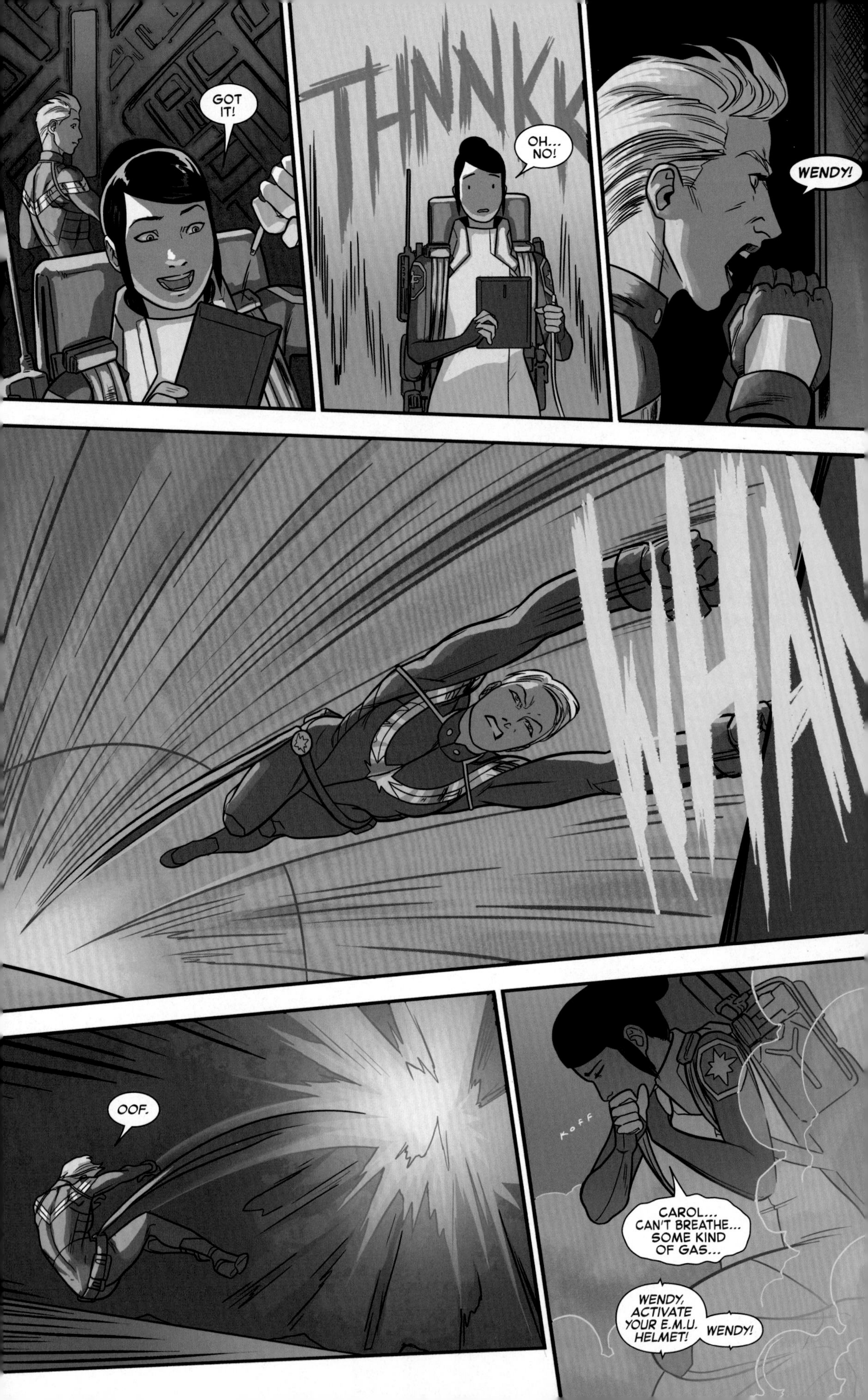
GOT IT!
THNNKK
OH... NO!
WENDY!
OOF.
KOFF
CAROL... CAN'T BREATHE... SOME KIND OF GAS...
WENDY, ACTIVATE YOUR E.M.U. HELMET!
WENDY!

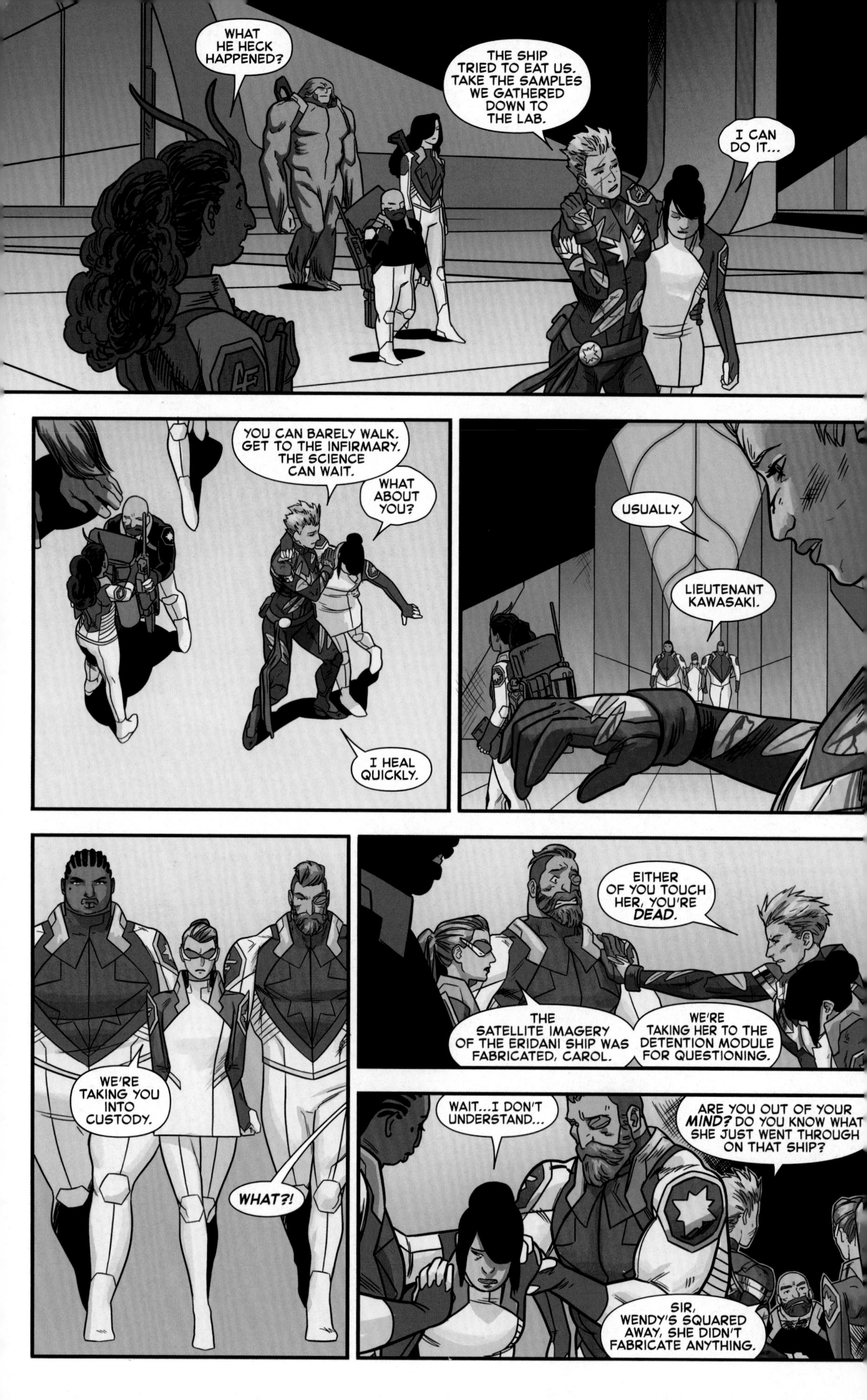
WHAT HE HECK HAPPENED?
THE SHIP TRIED TO EAT US. TAKE THE SAMPLES WE GATHERED DOWN TO THE LAB.
I CAN DO IT...
YOU CAN BARELY WALK. GET TO THE INFIRMARY. THE SCIENCE CAN WAIT.
WHAT ABOUT YOU?
I HEAL QUICKLY.
USUALLY.
LIEUTENANT KAWASAKI.
WE'RE TAKING YOU INTO CUSTODY.
WHAT?!
EITHER OF YOU TOUCH HER, YOU'RE *DEAD.*
THE SATELLITE IMAGERY OF THE ERIDANI SHIP WAS FABRICATED, CAROL.
WE'RE TAKING HER TO THE DETENTION MODULE FOR QUESTIONING.
WAIT...I DON'T UNDERSTAND...
ARE YOU OUT OF YOUR *MIND?* DO YOU KNOW WHAT SHE JUST WENT THROUGH ON THAT SHIP?
SIR, WENDY'S SQUARED AWAY, SHE DIDN'T FABRICATE ANYTHING.

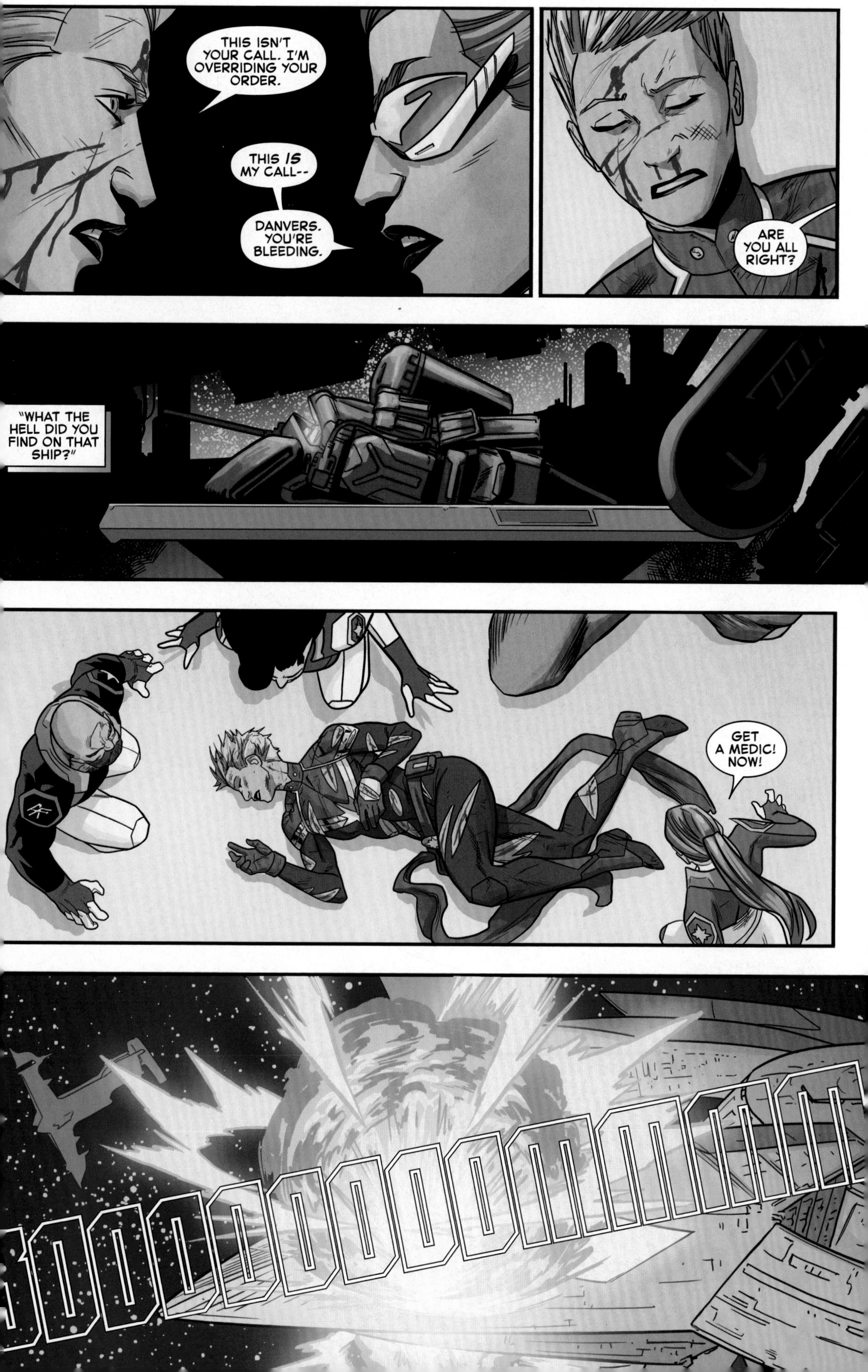
THIS ISN'T YOUR CALL. I'M OVERRIDING YOUR ORDER.
THIS *IS* MY CALL--
DANVERS. YOU'RE BLEEDING.
ARE YOU ALL RIGHT?
"WHAT THE HELL DID YOU FIND ON THAT SHIP?"
GET A MEDIC! NOW!
BOOOOOOOOOOMMMMM

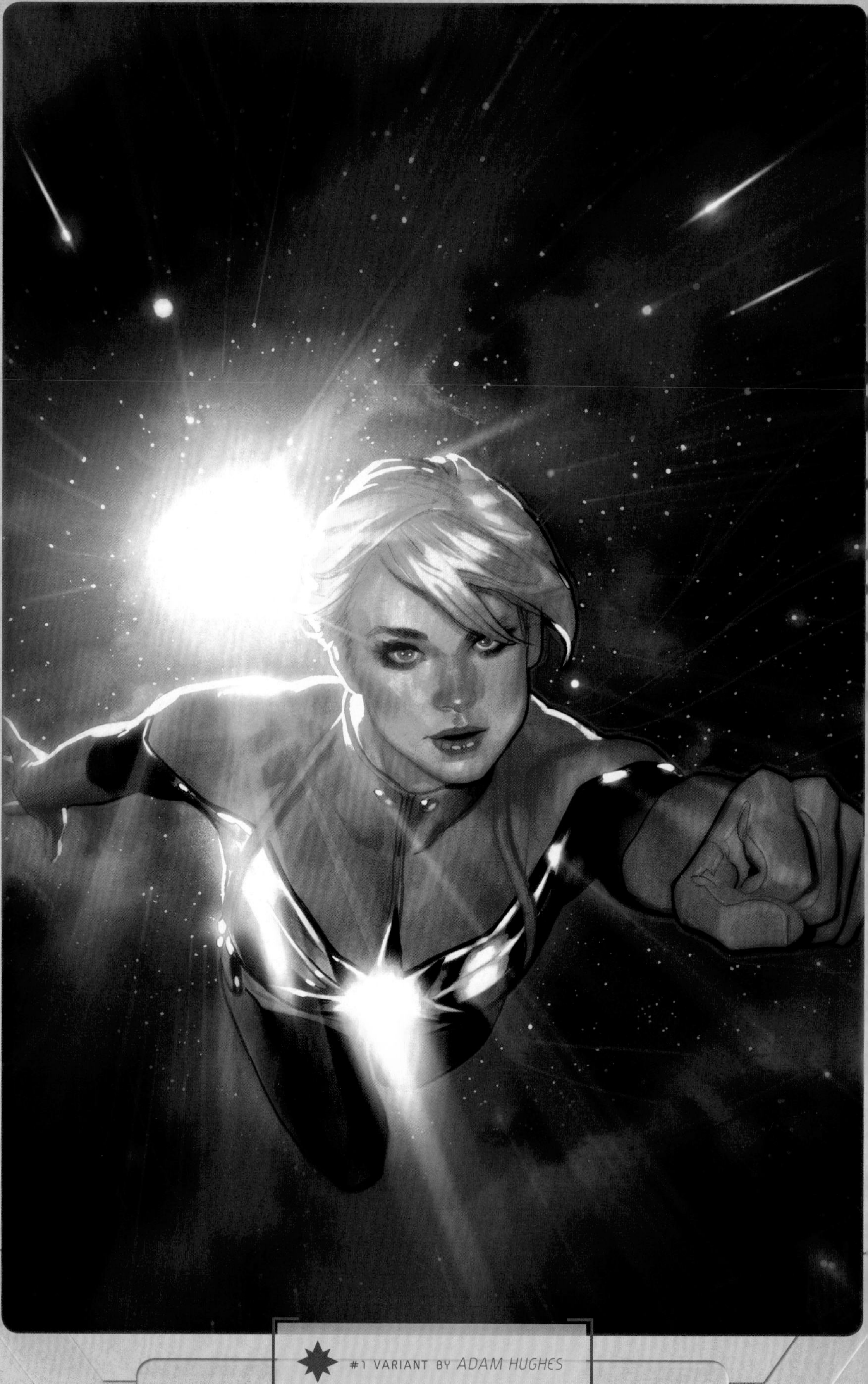

#1 VARIANT BY ADAM HUGHES

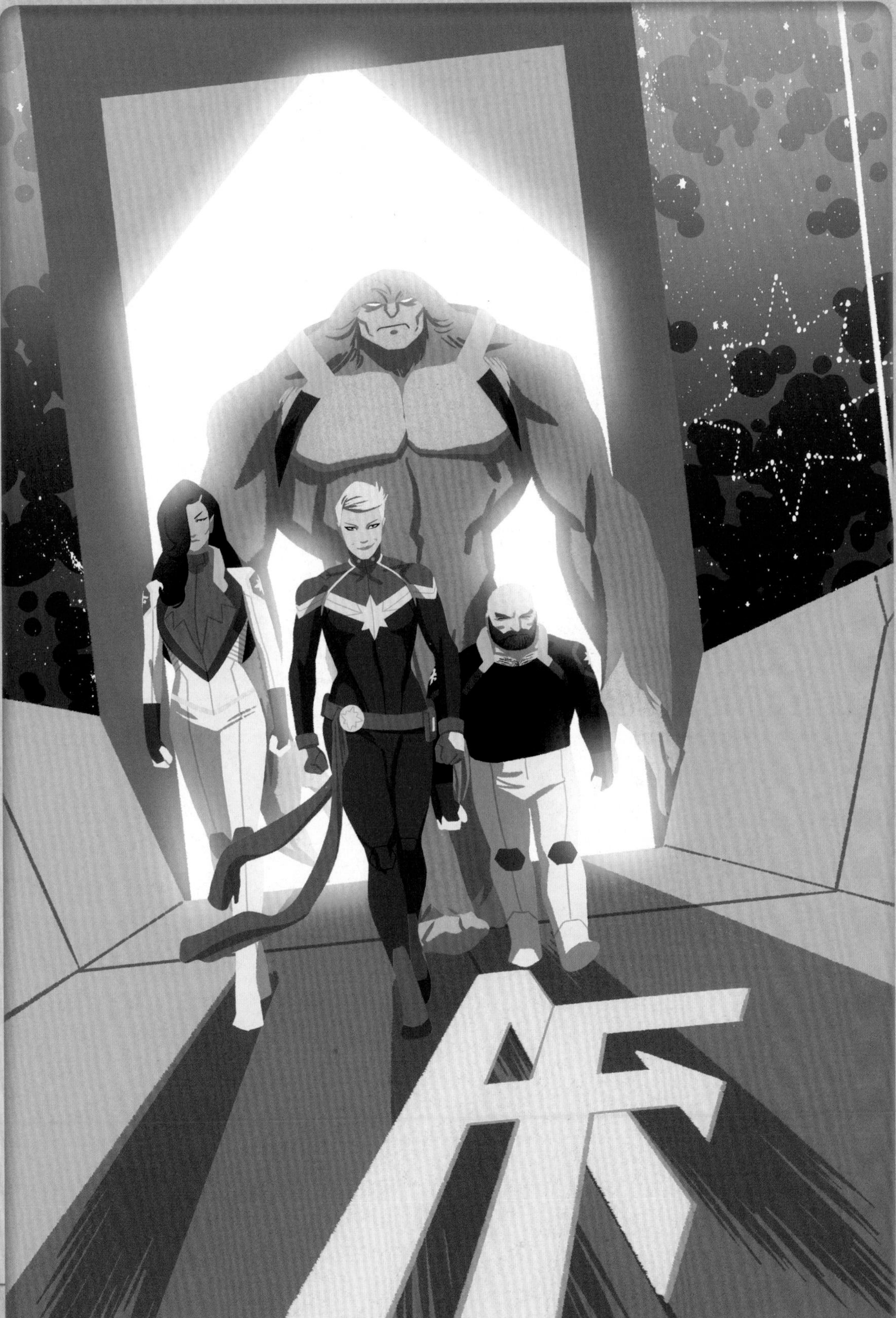

3

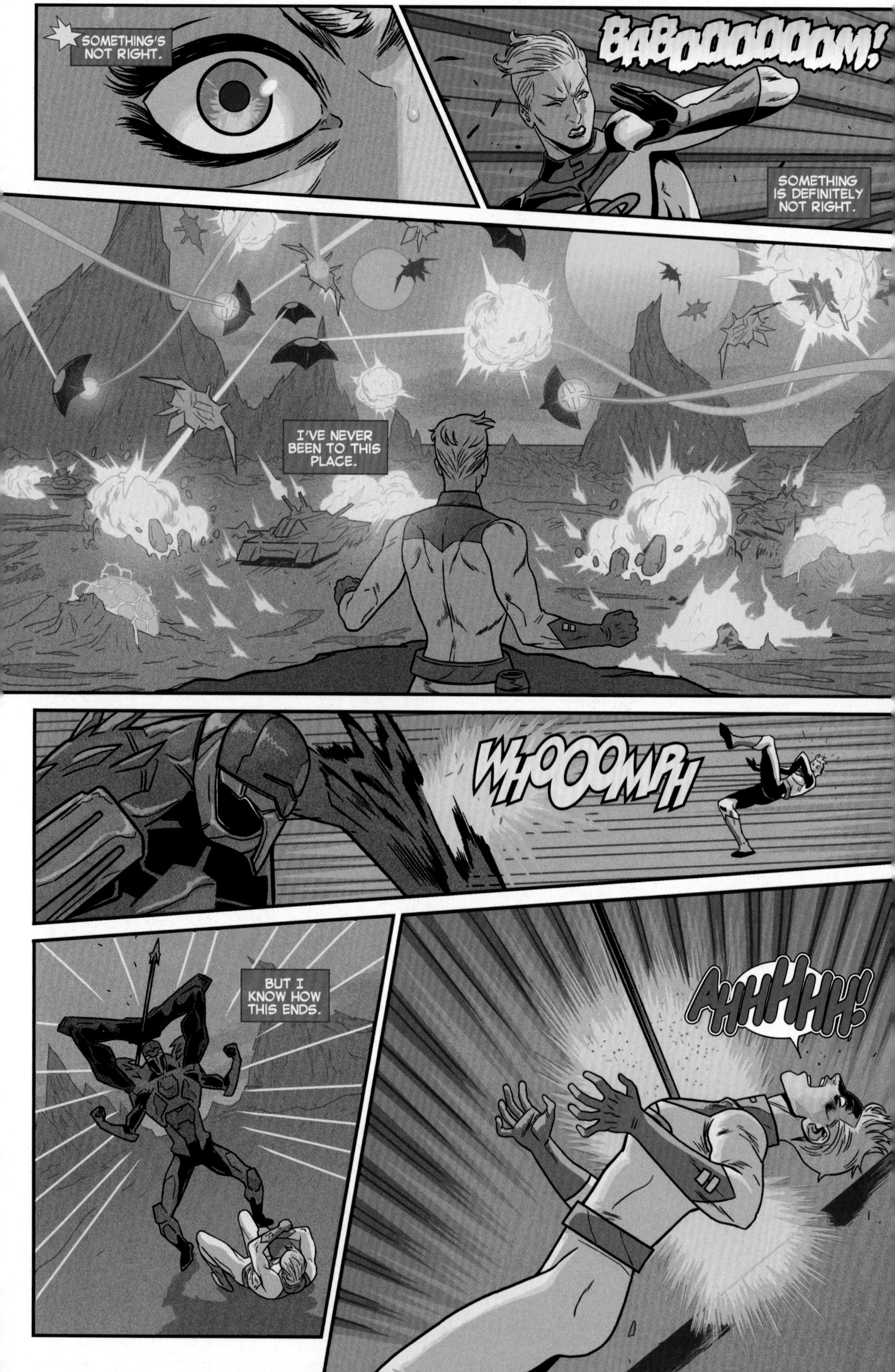
SOMETHING'S NOT RIGHT.
BABOOOOOOOM!
SOMETHING IS DEFINITELY NOT RIGHT.
I'VE NEVER BEEN TO THIS PLACE.
WHOOOOMPH
BUT I KNOW HOW THIS ENDS.
AHHHHH!

‹GASP›

GOTTA BE HONEST, THIS PLACE IS ONLY MARGINALLY BETTER.

GOOD, YOU'RE AWAKE.

HOW LONG HAVE I BEEN OUT?

TWELVE HOURS. HOW DO YOU FEEL?

I'M NOT SURE.

WELL, SOMETHING IS GOING ON WITH YOU. BUT I DON'T KNOW WHAT YET.

REASSURING.

YOUR IMMUNE SYSTEM IS WEAKENED. NOT JUST BY CAPTAIN MARVEL STANDARDS EITHER.

WHERE DO YOU THINK YOU'RE GOING?

YOU'RE NOT RELEASED. YOU HAVEN'T BEEN CLEARED FOR DUTY.

OKAY. GOOD TALK.

CAPTAIN!

WHICH MEANS I DIDN'T CAUSE THE EXPLOSION.

NO. WHATEVER YOU PUT IN YOUR BACKPACK DID.

WE WERE BRINGING THINGS BACK TO STUDY!

HOW'S YOUR BROTHER?

...WHAT?

I UNDERSTAND HE'S VERY ILL. MEDICAL BILLS MUST BE PILING UP.

YOU CAN'T... YOU *CAN'T* THINK--

TAKE A HIKE.

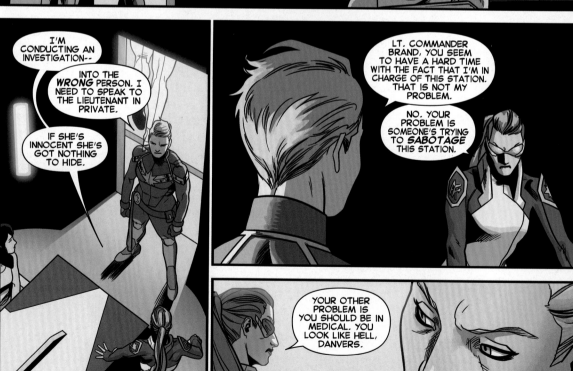

I'M CONDUCTING AN INVESTIGATION--

INTO THE *WRONG* PERSON. I NEED TO SPEAK TO THE LIEUTENANT IN PRIVATE.

IF SHE'S INNOCENT SHE'S GOT NOTHING TO HIDE.

LT. COMMANDER BRAND, YOU SEEM TO HAVE A HARD TIME WITH THE FACT THAT I'M IN CHARGE OF THIS STATION. THAT IS NOT MY PROBLEM.

NO. YOUR PROBLEM IS SOMEONE'S TRYING TO *SABOTAGE* THIS STATION.

YOUR OTHER PROBLEM IS YOU SHOULD BE IN MEDICAL. YOU LOOK LIKE HELL, DANVERS.

WHAT'S THE STATUS OF THE ALIEN VESSEL?

THIS IS THE DEVICE THAT DETONATED IN THE LAB. LOOKS PRETTY INTACT FOR A BOMB.

BECAUSE IT IS *REGENERATING* ITSELF.

NOTHING NEW. IT'S DOCKED OUTSIDE THE ALPHA FLIGHT MODULE.

ALSO STILL CREEPY.

A BOMB THAT REGENERATES ITSELF, AND WE THOUGHT IT WAS A GOOD PLAN TO BRING IT ONTO THE BRIDGE?

THAT'S WHAT *I* SAID.

IT'S NOT FULLY REGENERATED. AND ANY BLAST WOULD BE CONTAINED INSIDE THE FORCE FIELD.

WELL, I'M NOT TAKING ANY CHANCES. GET RID OF IT.

ZZZt
ZZZt

AND THEN WE'RE GETTING RID OF THIS.

RELEASE THE DOCKING CLAMPS ON THE VESSEL.

UNLESS YOU HAVE ANY OBJECTIONS.

FOR ONCE? NOPE.

CAPTAIN... THERE'S A PROBLEM.

THE DOCKING CLAMPS AREN'T RESPONDING. POWER LEVELS ARE NORMAL.

THEY'RE JUST... *STUCK.*

WANNA TRADE JOBS?

NOPE.

ALPHA FLIGHT MODULE.

WHAT THE *HELL* IS THAT?

IT APPEARS FROM THE ALIEN VESSEL HAS GROWN OVER THE DOCKING CLAMPS.

IT'S INFECTING THE STATION. LIKE CANCER.

WE NEED TO SEE HOW BAD THIS IS.

WHAT ARE YOU DOING?

TRYING TO...

...LOOK INSIDE...

...THIS WALL.

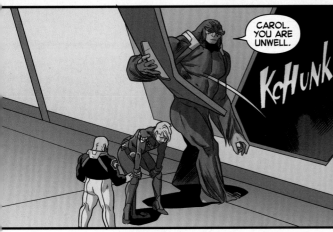

CAROL. YOU ARE UNWELL.

KCHUNK

SO'S THE STATION.

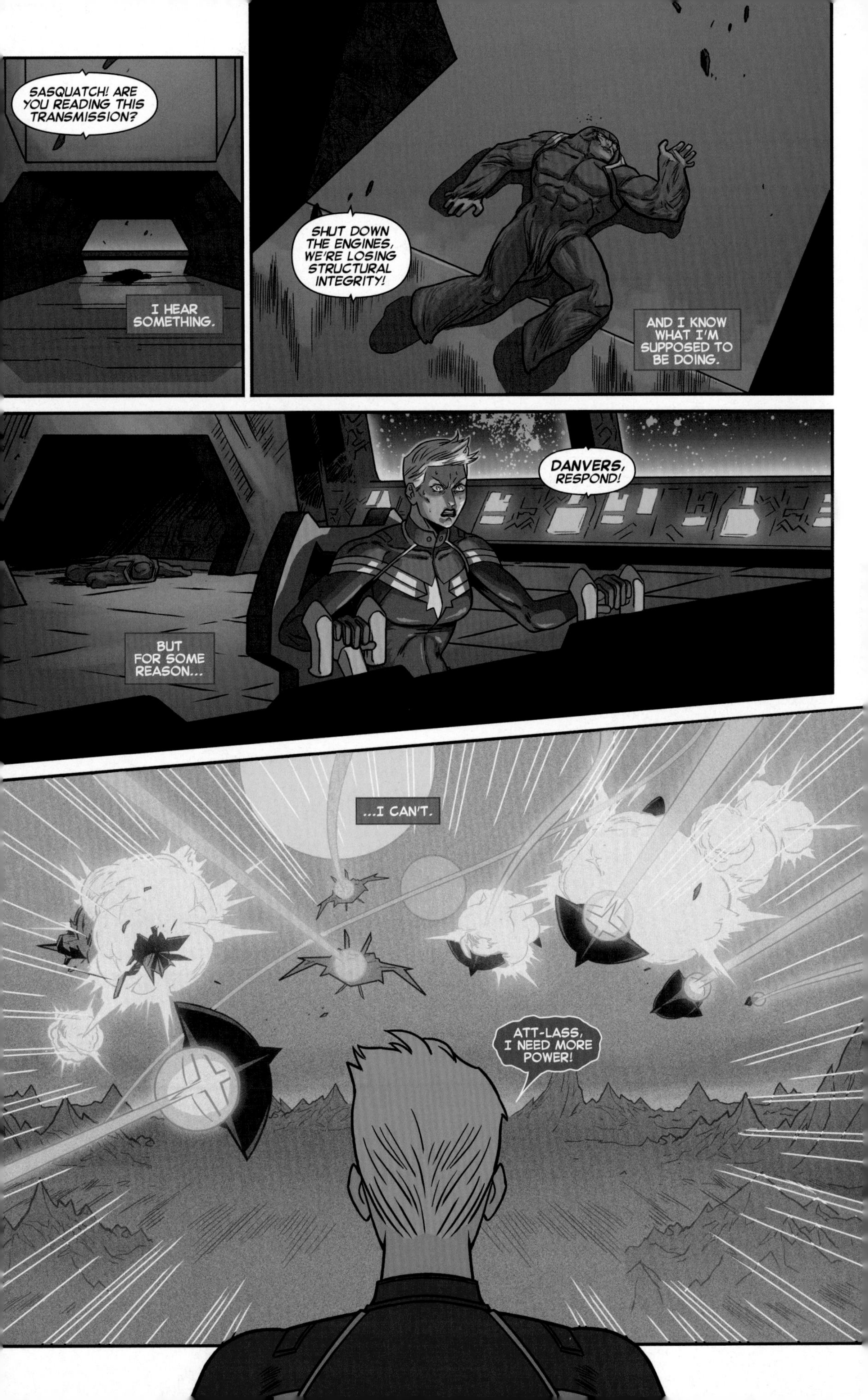
SASQUATCH! ARE YOU READING THIS TRANSMISSION?
I HEAR SOMETHING.
SHUT DOWN THE ENGINES, WE'RE LOSING STRUCTURAL INTEGRITY!
AND I KNOW WHAT I'M SUPPOSED TO BE DOING.
DANVERS, RESPOND!
BUT FOR SOME REASON...
...I CAN'T.
ATT-LASS, I NEED MORE POWER!

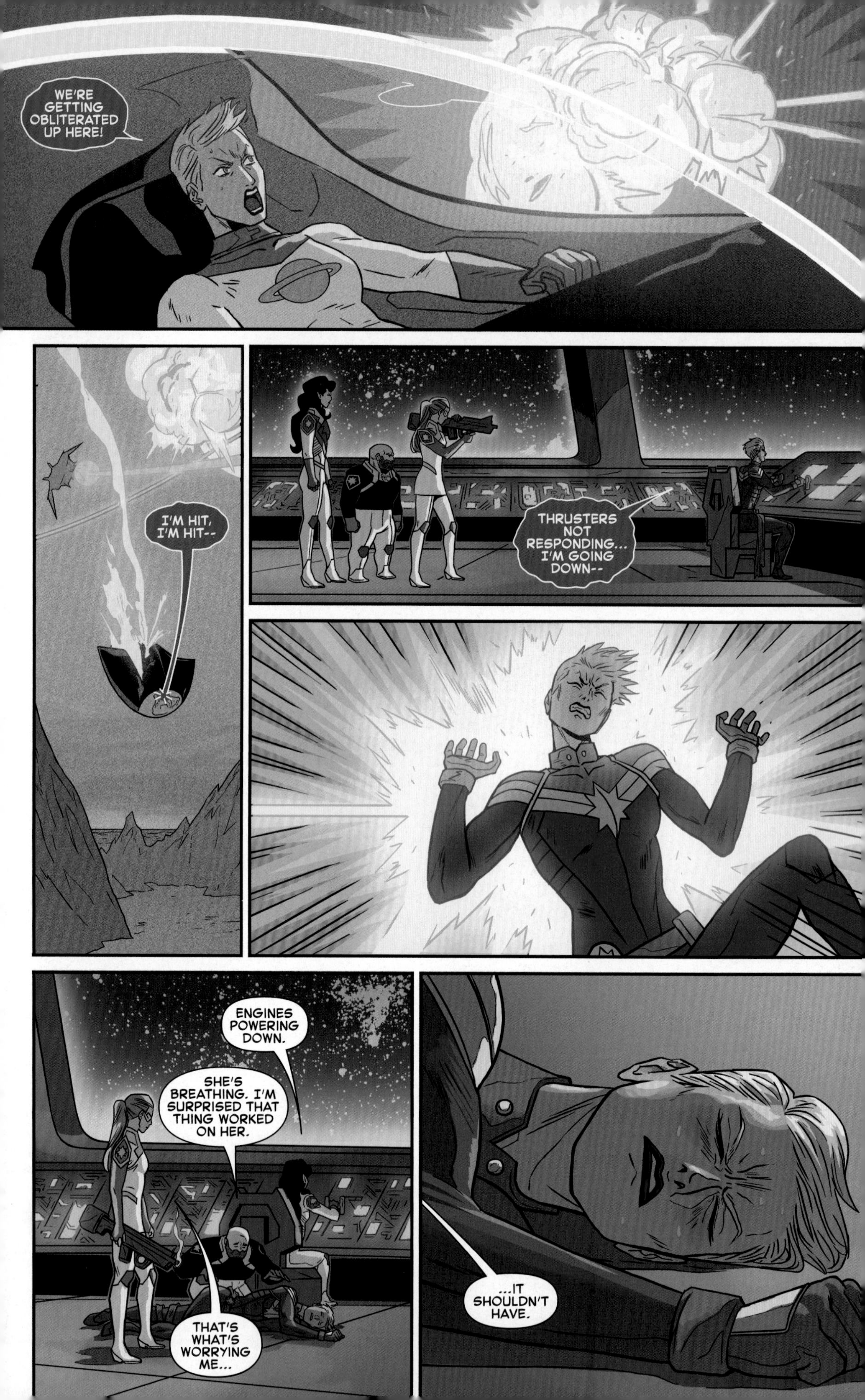
WE'RE GETTING OBLITERATED UP HERE!
I'M HIT, I'M HIT--
THRUSTERS NOT RESPONDING... I'M GOING DOWN--
ENGINES POWERING DOWN.
SHE'S BREATHING. I'M SURPRISED THAT THING WORKED ON HER.
THAT'S WHAT'S WORRYING ME...
...IT SHOULDN'T HAVE.

WAKE. UP.

WAKE. UP.

WAKE. UP.

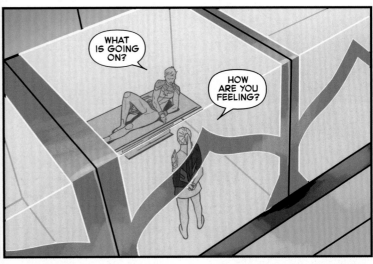

WHAT IS GOING ON?

HOW ARE YOU FEELING?

WHAT THE HELL ARE YOU TRYING TO PULL? WHY AM I IN DETENTION?

WHAT IS THE LAST THING YOU REMEMBER?

THE ALIEN SHIP... IT WAS GROWING INSIDE THE WALLS OF THE STATION. WALTER AND I BOARDED IT TO TRY AND PRY IT LOOSE.

YOU DON'T REMEMBER ATTACKING WALTER?

WHAT?

OR FIRING UP THE SHIP'S ENGINES WHILE IT WAS STILL DOCKED?

WHAT ARE YOU TALKING ABOUT?

YOU'VE BEEN HALLUCINATING, CAPTAIN. AND YOU'VE BECOME A DANGER TO US ALL.

LET ME OUT OF HERE.

NOT A CHANCE.

DO YOU REALLY THINK YOU CAN KEEP ME IN THIS CELL?

I DO. BECAUSE IN ADDITION TO HALLUCINATING, IT APPEARS YOUR POWERS HAVE BEEN DEPLETED.

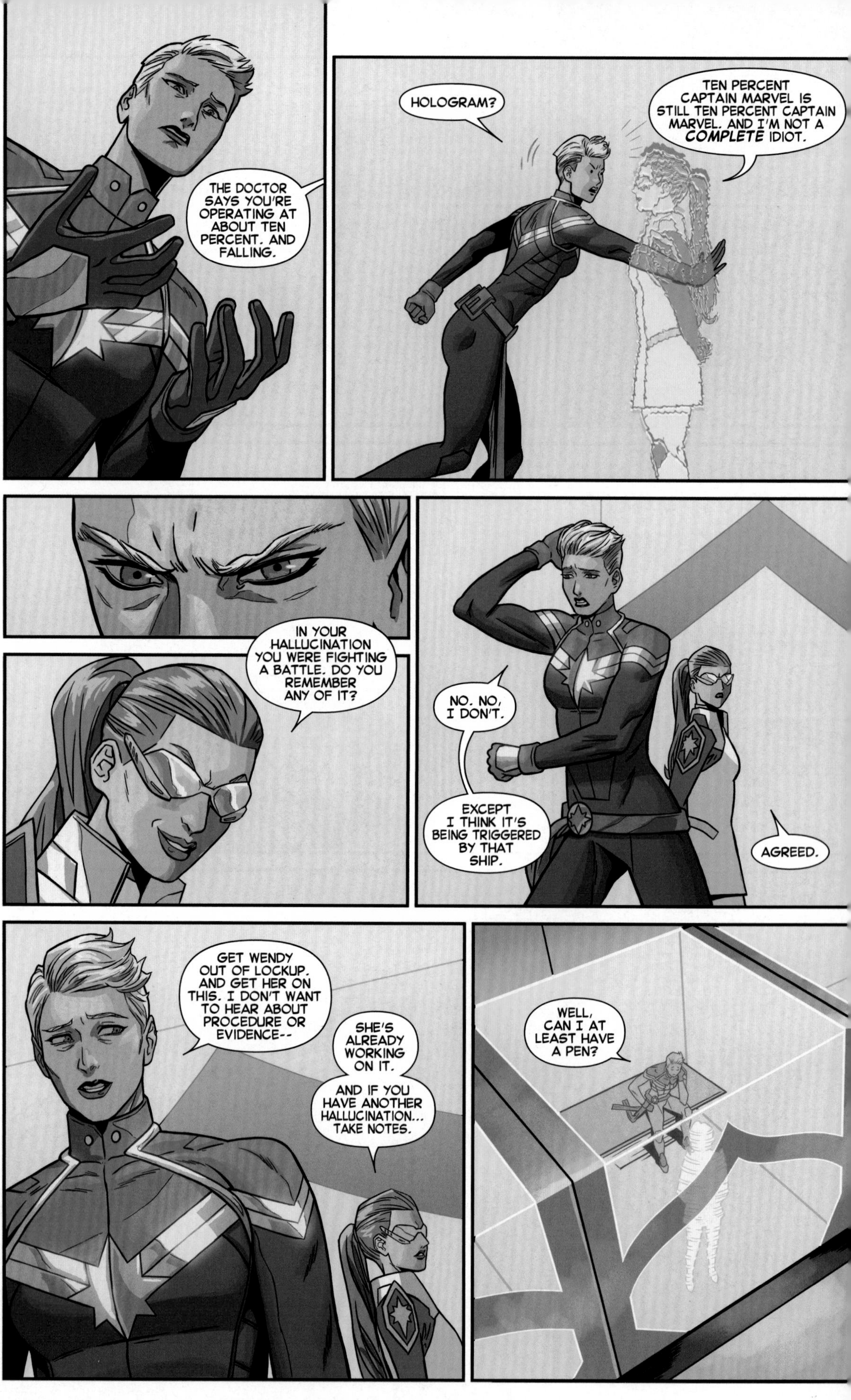
THE DOCTOR SAYS YOU'RE OPERATING AT ABOUT TEN PERCENT. AND FALLING.
HOLOGRAM?
TEN PERCENT CAPTAIN MARVEL IS STILL TEN PERCENT CAPTAIN MARVEL. AND I'M NOT A *COMPLETE* IDIOT.
IN YOUR HALLUCINATION YOU WERE FIGHTING A BATTLE. DO YOU REMEMBER ANY OF IT?
NO. NO, I DON'T.
EXCEPT I THINK IT'S BEING TRIGGERED BY THAT SHIP.
AGREED.
GET WENDY OUT OF LOCKUP. AND GET HER ON THIS. I DON'T WANT TO HEAR ABOUT PROCEDURE OR EVIDENCE--
SHE'S ALREADY WORKING ON IT.
AND IF YOU HAVE ANOTHER HALLUCINATION... TAKE NOTES.
WELL, CAN I AT LEAST HAVE A PEN?

LOOK AT THIS STUFF. NOT A SCRATCH ON ANYTHING. YOU'D NEVER KNOW IT'D BEEN BLOWN TO SMITHEREENS.

THE COMPOUND REGENERATES TWENTY TIMES FASTER THAN A HUMAN LIVER.

I'M SORRY YOUR SLUG DIDN'T REGENERATE.

UH-HUH.

I'D OFFER TO GET YOU ANOTHER ONE, BUT I CAN'T.

BECAUSE SLUGS.

I'M NOT HELPING, AM I?

LOOK AT THAT PATTERN. IT'S ALL OVER THEIR MAIN COMPUTER. THIS MEANS SOMETHING. I JUST DON'T KNOW WHAT.

AND THERE ARE TWENTY-TWO OTHER PATTERNS THAT ARE SIMILAR. ALL REPEATING TOGETHER.

CHROMOSOMES.

HUMANOIDS HAVE TWENTY-THREE CHROMOSOMES.

THE COMPUTER CAN GIVE US A GRAPHIC REPRESENTATION OF THE CODE.

IT'S DNA.

WHOSE?

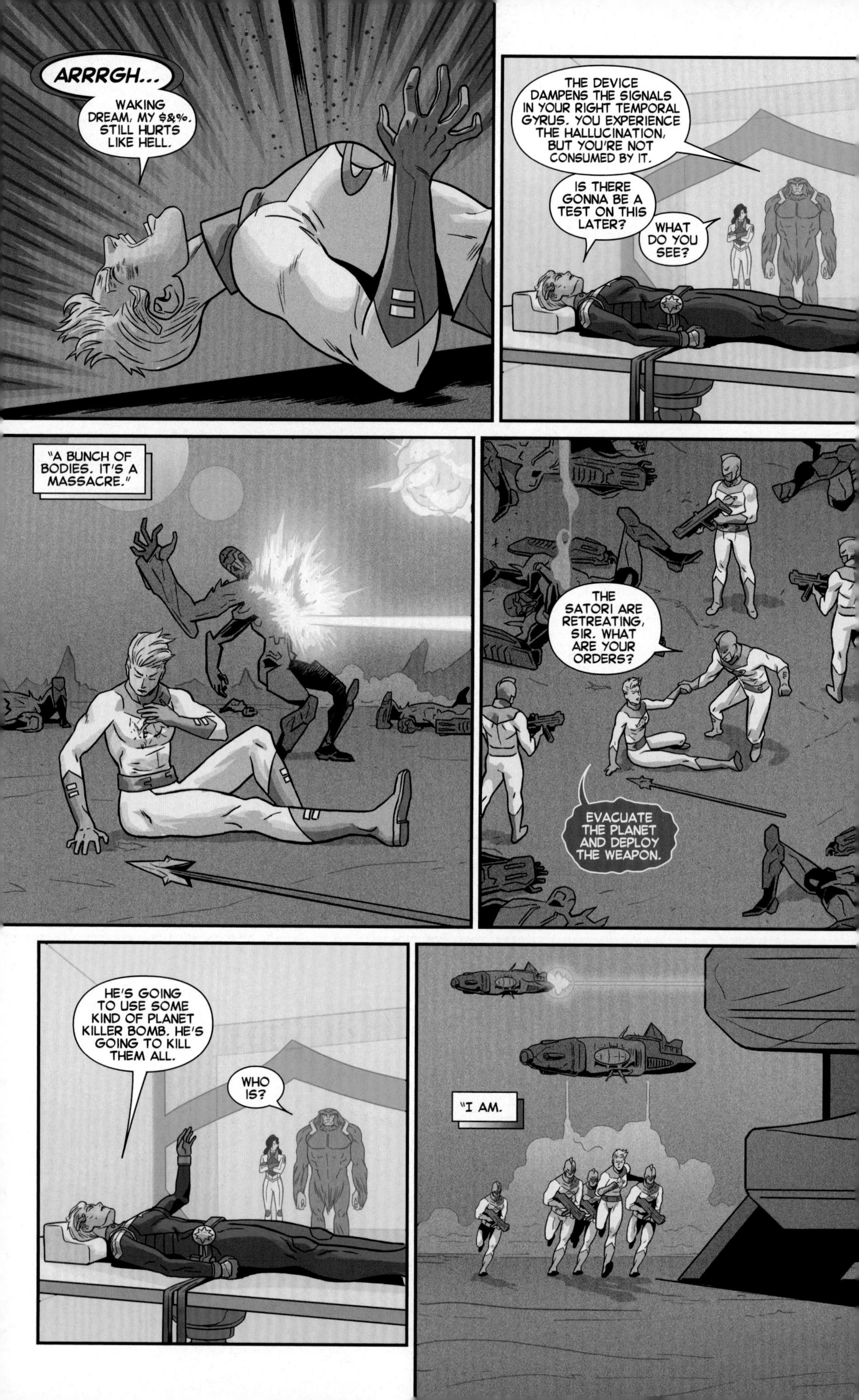
ARRRGH...
WAKING DREAM, MY $&%. STILL HURTS LIKE HELL.
THE DEVICE DAMPENS THE SIGNALS IN YOUR RIGHT TEMPORAL GYRUS. YOU EXPERIENCE THE HALLUCINATION, BUT YOU'RE NOT CONSUMED BY IT.
IS THERE GONNA BE A TEST ON THIS LATER?
WHAT DO YOU SEE?
"A BUNCH OF BODIES. IT'S A MASSACRE."
THE SATORI ARE RETREATING, SIR. WHAT ARE YOUR ORDERS?
EVACUATE THE PLANET AND DEPLOY THE WEAPON.
HE'S GOING TO USE SOME KIND OF PLANET KILLER BOMB. HE'S GOING TO KILL THEM ALL.
WHO IS?
"I AM.

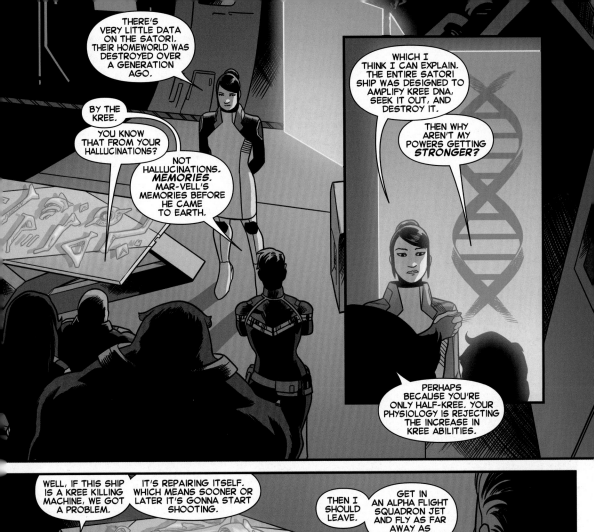

THERE'S VERY LITTLE DATA ON THE SATORI. THEIR HOMEWORLD WAS DESTROYED OVER A GENERATION AGO.

BY THE KREE.

YOU KNOW THAT FROM YOUR HALLUCINATIONS?

NOT HALLUCINATIONS. MEMORIES. MAR-VELL'S MEMORIES BEFORE HE CAME TO EARTH.

WHICH I THINK I CAN EXPLAIN. THE ENTIRE SATORI SHIP WAS DESIGNED TO AMPLIFY KREE DNA, SEEK IT OUT, AND DESTROY IT.

THEN WHY AREN'T MY POWERS GETTING STRONGER?

PERHAPS BECAUSE YOU'RE ONLY HALF-KREE. YOUR PHYSIOLOGY IS REJECTING THE INCREASE IN KREE ABILITIES.

WELL, IF THIS SHIP IS A KREE KILLING MACHINE, WE GOT A PROBLEM.

IT'S REPAIRING ITSELF. WHICH MEANS SOONER OR LATER IT'S GONNA START SHOOTING.

THEN I SHOULD LEAVE.

GET IN AN ALPHA FLIGHT SQUADRON JET AND FLY AS FAR AWAY AS POSSIBLE.

THE SATORI SHIP IS STILL ENTANGLED WITH THE STATION. ONCE IT AWAKENS, IT WILL STILL TRY TO PURSUE YOU.

TEARING THE STATION APART IN THE PROCESS.

THEN LET'S PULL IT APART OURSELVES.

THE STATION WAS DESIGNED TO BE MODULAR. NEED A BETTER SCIENCE DEPARTMENT? JUST SWAP OUT THE OLD MODULE WITH A NEW ONE.

SO WE'RE JUST GOING TO TAKE THE ENTIRE ALPHA FLIGHT MODULE *OFF* THE STATION?

AFTER WE'VE MOVED OUT THE SQUADRON AND WHATEVER ISN'T NAILED DOWN.

WHERE IS LT. COMMANDER BRAND?

EUGENE, YOU HAVE EYES ON BRAND?

HAVEN'T SEEN HER.

WE'RE GOOD TO GO DOWN HERE, CAP. WHAT'S THE PLAN AFTER WE DISCONNECT THE MODULE?

I THOUGHT I'D STRAP A ROCKET TO IT AND LAUNCH IT TOWARD THE CENTER OF THE SUN.

HELL. YES.

SHOULD ONLY COST A HUNDRED BILLION DOLLARS TO REPLACE.

WE CAN'T WAIT FOR BRAND. LET'S DO THIS. ON MY MARK... *NOW.*

ALPHA FLIGHT MODULE IS AWAY.

CAPTAIN... CAROL.

BRAND'S BEEN ATTACKED. WALTER FOUND HER. SHE'S IN MEDICAL.

CAPTAIN MARVEL, WE HAVE A NEW CONTACT ON LONG-RANGE SENSORS.

WHAT?

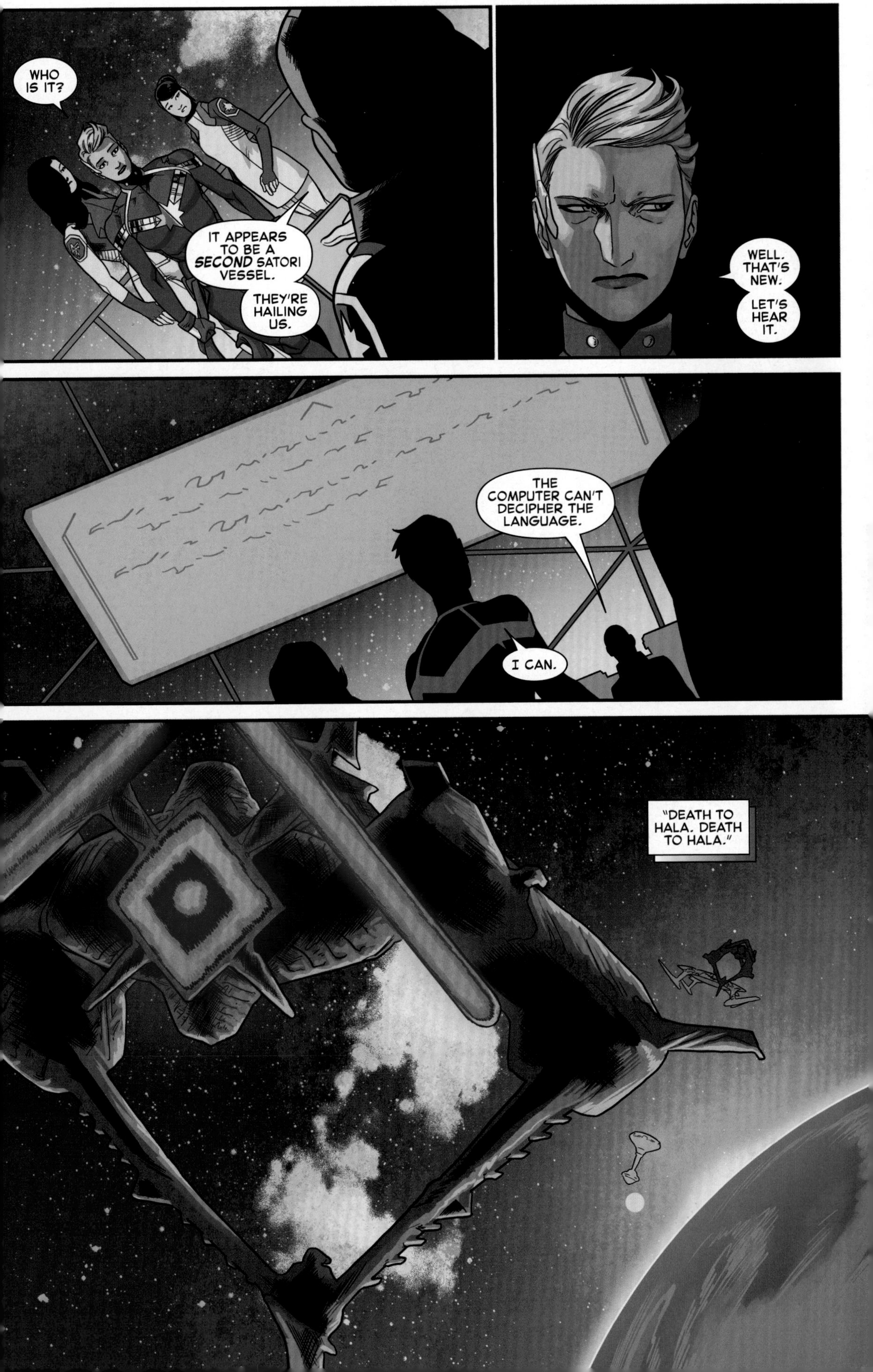
WHO IS IT?
IT APPEARS TO BE A SECOND SATORI VESSEL.
THEY'RE HAILING US.
WELL. THAT'S NEW.
LET'S HEAR IT.
THE COMPUTER CAN'T DECIPHER THE LANGUAGE.
I CAN.
"DEATH TO HALA. DEATH TO HALA."

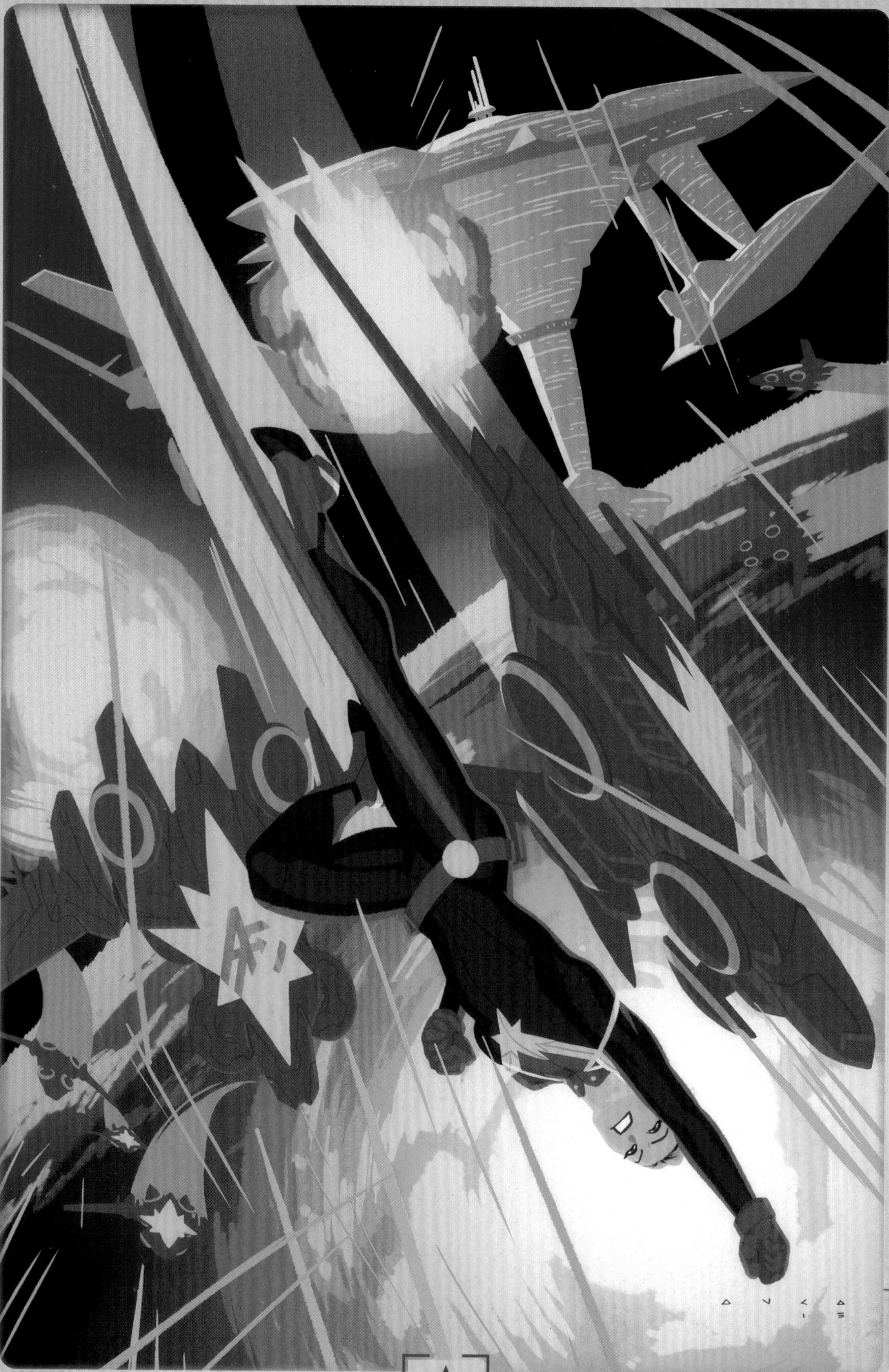

ROCKET RACCOON, GUARDIANS of the GALAXY.

...OTHER INTO THE SECURITY SYSTEM OF ULTIMATES HQ AT THE TRISKELION.

AND IT'S SPREADING TO OTHER BASES.

GUARDIANS HAVEN'T SEEN IT YET. BUT I HAVEN'T OPENED MY EMAIL IN... EVER.

UNFORTUNATELY THAT'S NOT OUR ONLY PROBLEM. THE LAST DATA TRANSMISSION FROM AFSS HAD A VIRUS HIDDEN IN THE CODE. REAL NASTY ONE, TOO.

DEFINE NASTY.

THE TRANSMISSION CAME FROM YOU, LT. COMMANDER BRAND.

NO. IT DIDN'T.

THEY GOT INTO MY COMPUTER.

NOW WE KNOW WHY.

YOU THINK IT WAS WHOEVER ATTACKED BRAND.

HAS TO BE.

HE'S GETTING BOLD.

OR DESPERATE.

WISH GUARDIANS COULD BE USEFUL. PEDAL TO THE METAL, WE'RE STILL TWO HOURS FROM RENDEZVOUSING WITH YOU.

AND YOU WITHOUT YOUR POWERS--

IT'S ALL RIGHT, I'VE GOT A PLAN TO DEAL WITH THAT PROBLEM. I SHOULD BE 100 PERCENT AFTER WE DESTROY THE SATORI GHOST SHIP...

OH... DO I NEED PERMISSION TO BLOW UP THE ALPHA FLIGHT MODULE?

I'M NOT THE ONE TO ASK, BUT SURE. GRANTED.

GOOD LUCK, CAPTAIN.

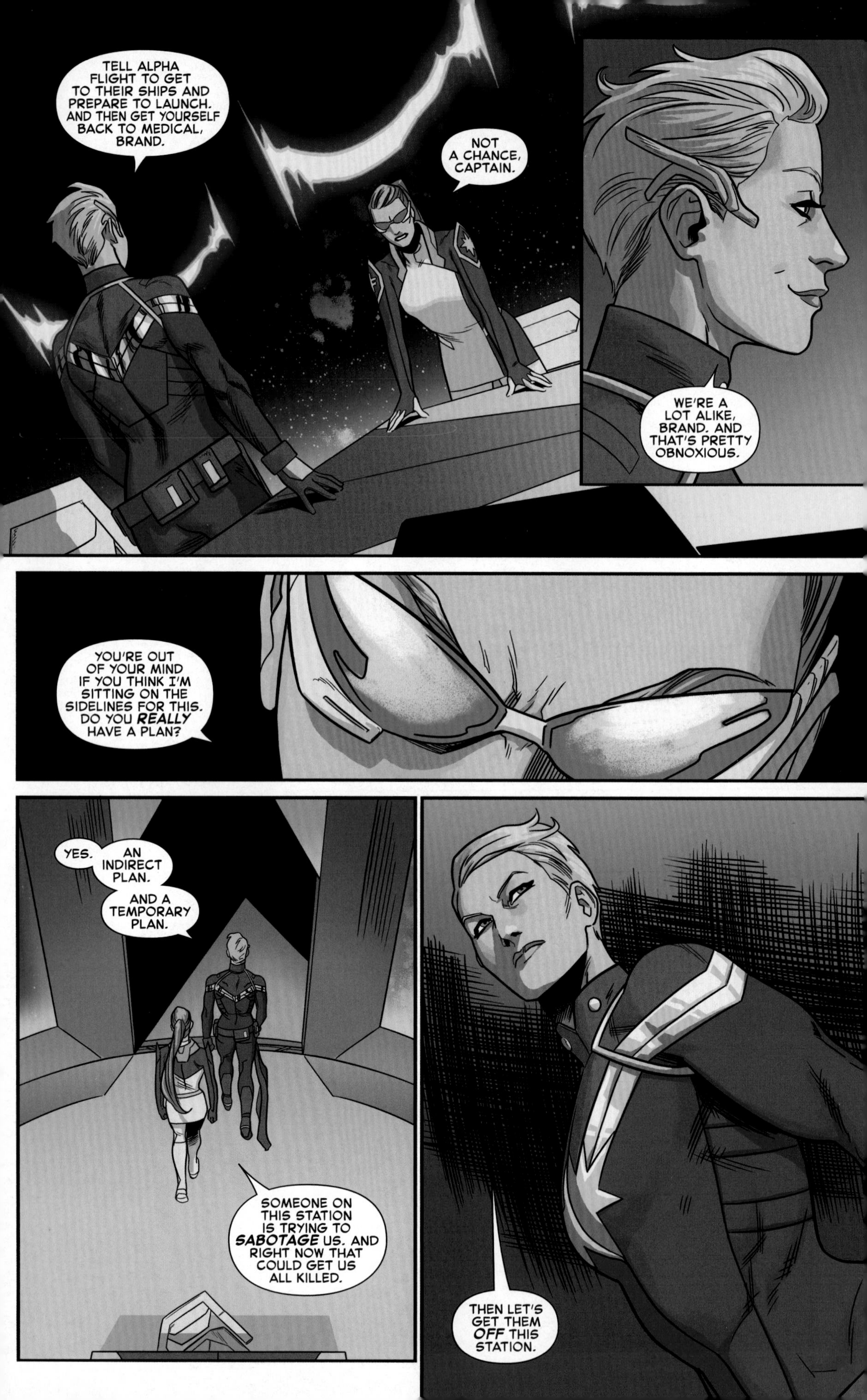
TELL ALPHA FLIGHT TO GET TO THEIR SHIPS AND PREPARE TO LAUNCH. AND THEN GET YOURSELF BACK TO MEDICAL, BRAND.
NOT A CHANCE, CAPTAIN.
WE'RE A LOT ALIKE, BRAND. AND THAT'S PRETTY OBNOXIOUS.
YOU'RE OUT OF YOUR MIND IF YOU THINK I'M SITTING ON THE SIDELINES FOR THIS. DO YOU *REALLY* HAVE A PLAN?
YES.
AN INDIRECT PLAN.
AND A TEMPORARY PLAN.
SOMEONE ON THIS STATION IS TRYING TO *SABOTAGE* US. AND RIGHT NOW THAT COULD GET US ALL KILLED.
THEN LET'S GET THEM *OFF* THIS STATION.

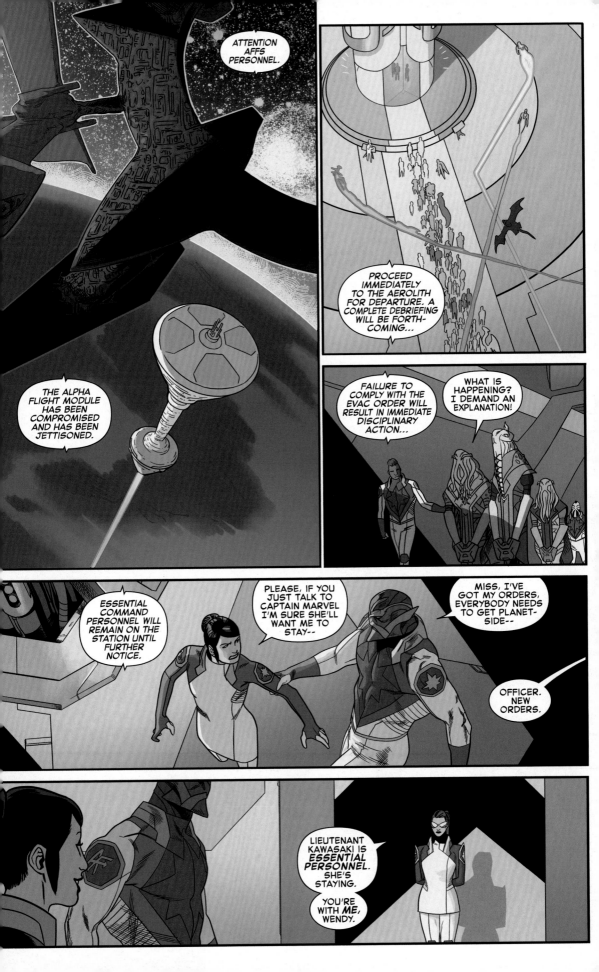

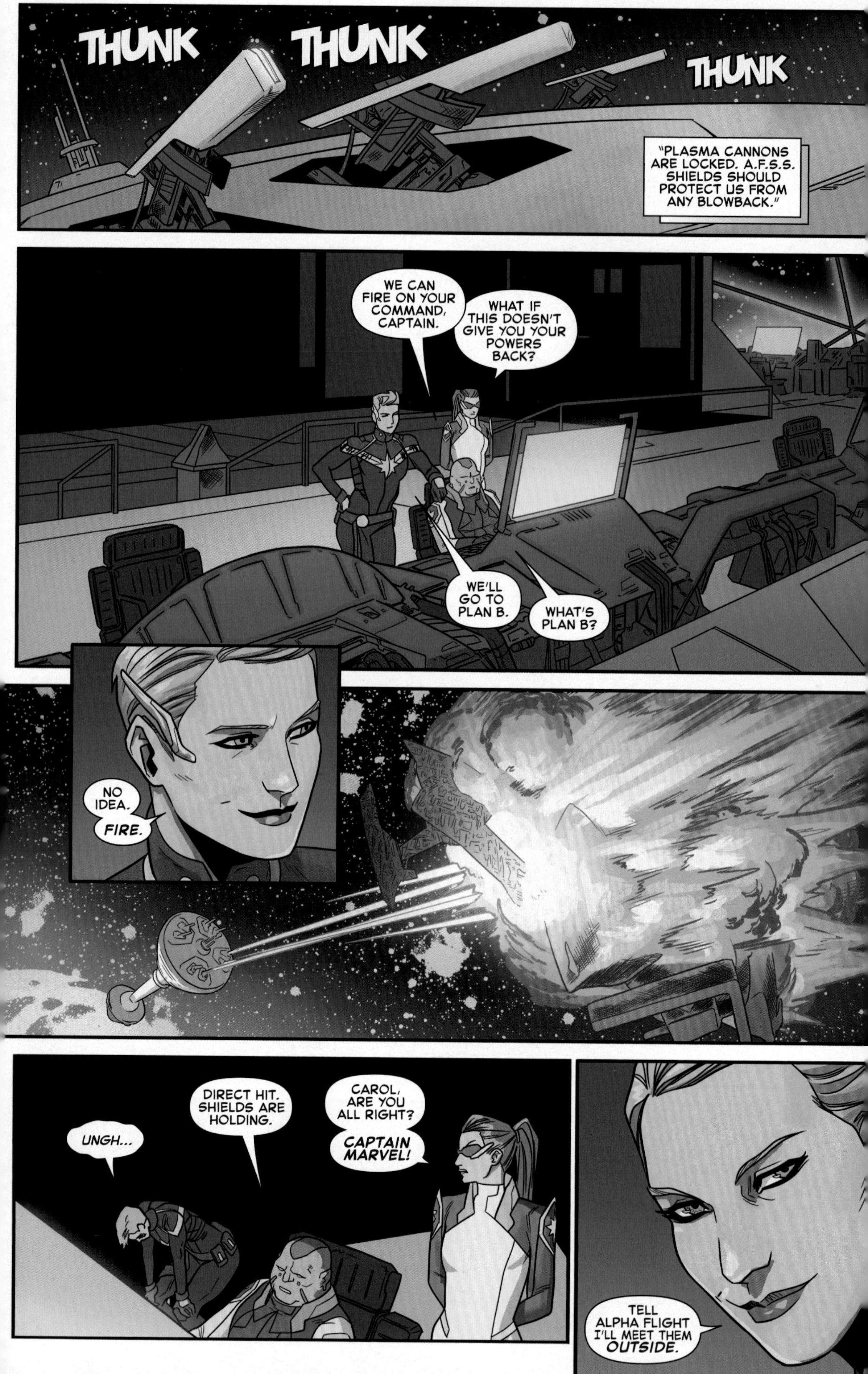
THUNK
THUNK
THUNK
"PLASMA CANNONS ARE LOCKED. A.F.S.S. SHIELDS SHOULD PROTECT US FROM ANY BLOWBACK."
WE CAN FIRE ON YOUR COMMAND, CAPTAIN.
WHAT IF THIS DOESN'T GIVE YOU YOUR POWERS BACK?
WE'LL GO TO PLAN B.
WHAT'S PLAN B?
NO IDEA. FIRE.
UNGH...
DIRECT HIT. SHIELDS ARE HOLDING.
CAROL, ARE YOU ALL RIGHT? CAPTAIN MARVEL!
TELL ALPHA FLIGHT I'LL MEET THEM OUTSIDE.

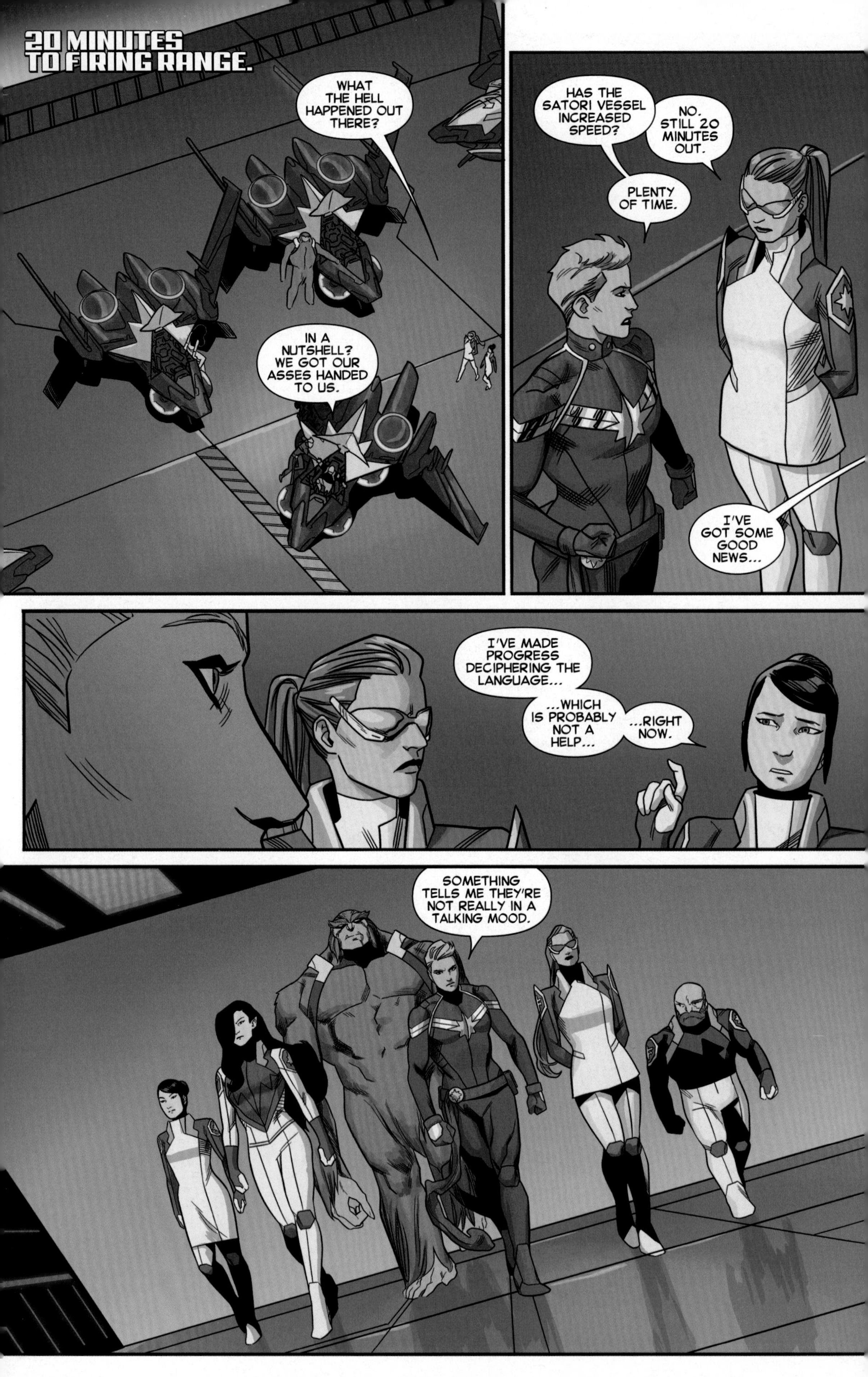
20 MINUTES TO FIRING RANGE.
WHAT THE HELL HAPPENED OUT THERE?
IN A NUTSHELL? WE GOT OUR ASSES HANDED TO US.
HAS THE SATORI VESSEL INCREASED SPEED?
NO. STILL 20 MINUTES OUT.
PLENTY OF TIME.
I'VE GOT SOME GOOD NEWS...
I'VE MADE PROGRESS DECIPHERING THE LANGUAGE...
...WHICH IS PROBABLY NOT A HELP...
...RIGHT NOW.
SOMETHING TELLS ME THEY'RE NOT REALLY IN A TALKING MOOD.

I'VE GOT SOME EXPERIENCE IN LINGUISTICS. I COULD HELP WENDY SPEED UP THE TRANSLATION PROCESS.

SEEMS LIKE WE'RE PAST THAT NOW.

THINK OF A PLAN B YET?

YEAH. EVACUATE YOURSELVES. I'LL HANDLE THEM MYSELF.

THAT'S NOT A PLAN. THAT'S *SUICIDE*.

RIGHT NOW THE ONLY THING WE'VE GOT GOING FOR US IS THAT THEY'VE GOT ONE TARGET: ME. SO LET'S GIVE THEM WHAT THEY WANT.

I'M SORRY, CAPTAIN. I'M NOT DOING THAT.

ME NEITHER.

UNDER NO CIRCUMSTANCES.

I AM GIVING YOU ALL A *DIRECT ORDER*--

TELL IT TO THE MARINES.

HONESTLY, I COULD GO EITHER WAY.

BREEEE BREEEE BREEE

OH, THAT'S A HAPPY SOUND.

ALL RIGHT. SO MY PLAN B STINKS. ANYBODY ELSE HAVE A BRIGHT IDEA?

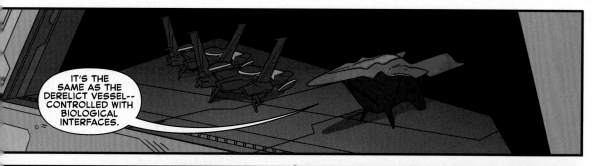

IT'S THE SAME AS THE DERELICT VESSEL-- CONTROLLED WITH BIOLOGICAL INTERFACES.

EUGENE, PLACE YOUR HAND INSIDE THAT VISCOUS MATERIAL.

SOUNDS SUPER SEXY WHEN YOU SAY THAT.

YOU'RE REPULSIVE.

THIS IS WEIRD. BUT IN A GOOD WAY.

WHAT DO YOU FEEL?

LIKE LITTLE PINS AND NEEDLES, SOME SORT OF CURRENT.

CAN YOU CONTROL ANY OF THE SHIP'S FUNCTIONS?

TRYING. I DON'T THINK I CAN.

WEAPONS. SHIELDS. ENGINES.

YOU'VE MADE PROGRESS WITH THE LANGUAGE.

THIS IS INTERESTING.

IT'S CONNECTED TO THE SHIP. EVEN NOW. LIKE SOME SORT OF BIOMETRIC SATELLITE.

WHICH MEANS WE'VE BEEN GOING ABOUT THIS THE WRONG WAY. WE CAN'T BEAT IT FROM THE OUTSIDE.

SO, LET'S KILL IT FROM THE INSIDE.

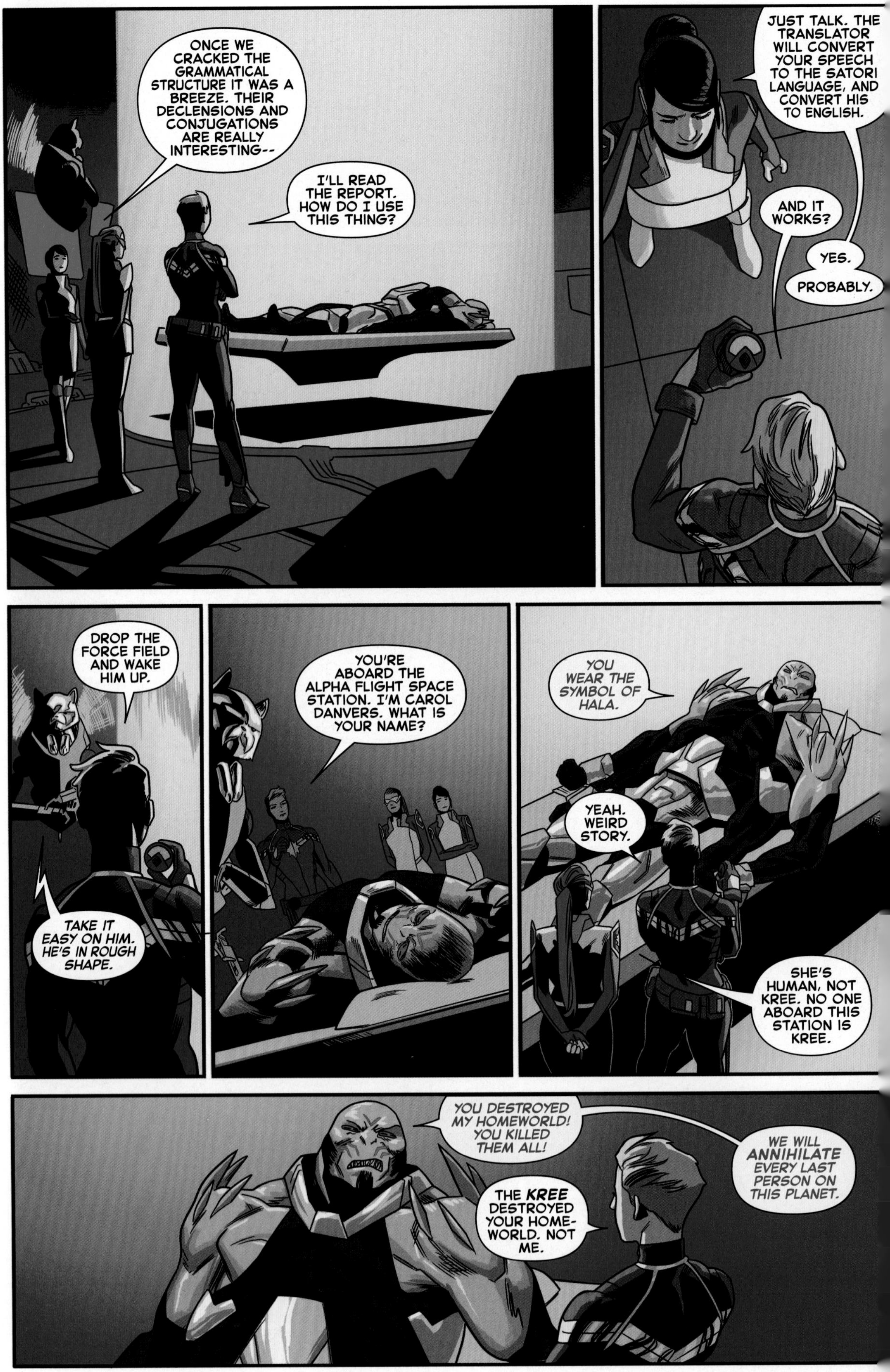
ONCE WE CRACKED THE GRAMMATICAL STRUCTURE IT WAS A BREEZE. THEIR DECLENSIONS AND CONJUGATIONS ARE REALLY INTERESTING--
I'LL READ THE REPORT. HOW DO I USE THIS THING?
JUST TALK. THE TRANSLATOR WILL CONVERT YOUR SPEECH TO THE SATORI LANGUAGE, AND CONVERT HIS TO ENGLISH.
AND IT WORKS?
YES.
PROBABLY.
DROP THE FORCE FIELD AND WAKE HIM UP.
TAKE IT EASY ON HIM. HE'S IN ROUGH SHAPE.
YOU'RE ABOARD THE ALPHA FLIGHT SPACE STATION. I'M CAROL DANVERS. WHAT IS YOUR NAME?
YOU WEAR THE SYMBOL OF HALA.
YEAH. WEIRD STORY.
SHE'S HUMAN, NOT KREE. NO ONE ABOARD THIS STATION IS KREE.
YOU DESTROYED MY HOMEWORLD! YOU KILLED THEM ALL!
THE KREE DESTROYED YOUR HOME-WORLD. NOT ME.
WE WILL ANNIHILATE EVERY LAST PERSON ON THIS PLANET.

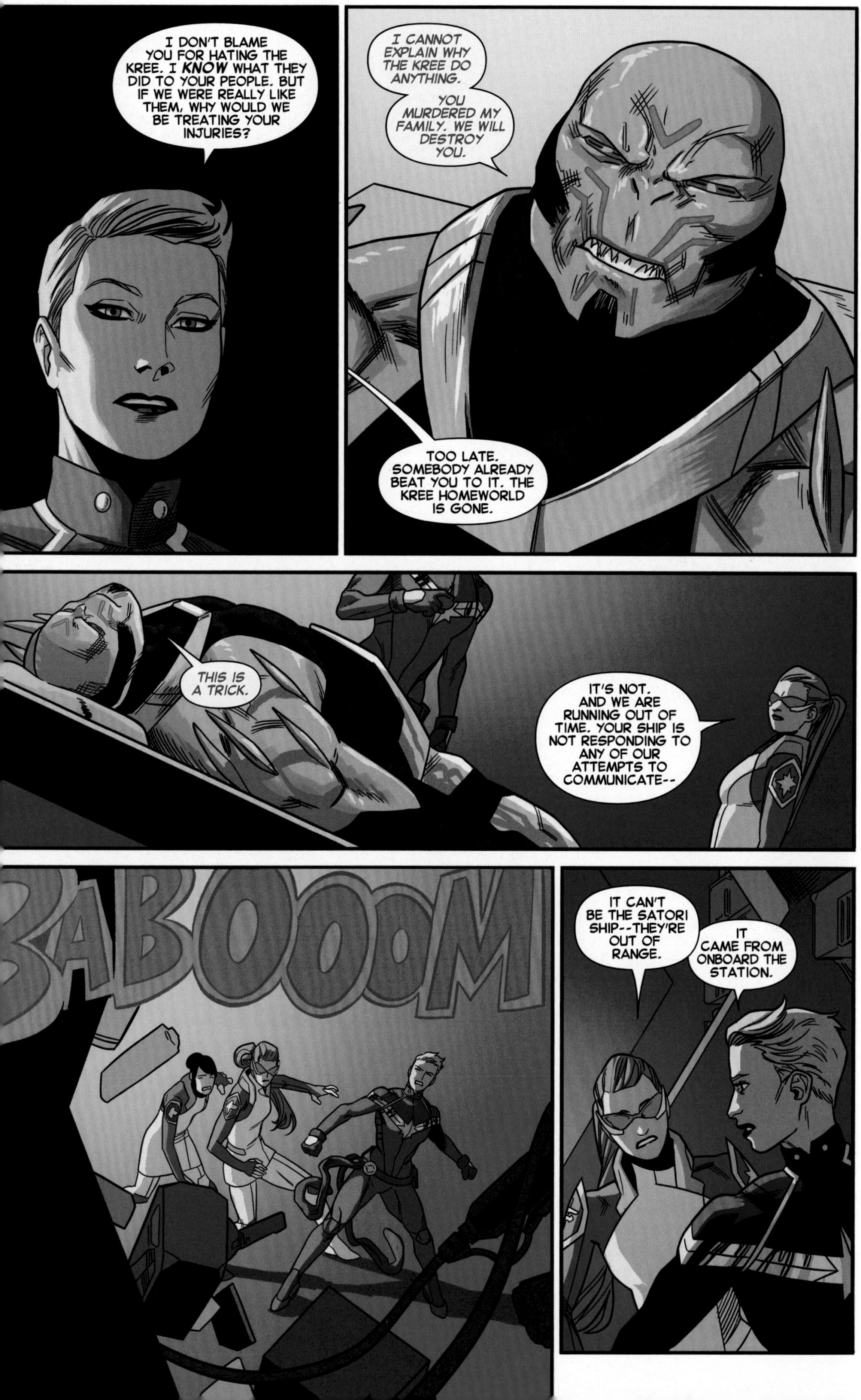
I DON'T BLAME YOU FOR HATING THE KREE. I **KNOW** WHAT THEY DID TO YOUR PEOPLE. BUT IF WE WERE REALLY LIKE THEM, WHY WOULD WE BE TREATING YOUR INJURIES?
I CANNOT EXPLAIN WHY THE KREE DO ANYTHING.
YOU MURDERED MY FAMILY. WE WILL DESTROY YOU.
TOO LATE. SOMEBODY ALREADY BEAT YOU TO IT. THE KREE HOMEWORLD IS GONE.
THIS IS A TRICK.
IT'S NOT. AND WE ARE RUNNING OUT OF TIME. YOUR SHIP IS NOT RESPONDING TO ANY OF OUR ATTEMPTS TO COMMUNICATE--
BABOOOM
IT CAN'T BE THE SATORI SHIP--THEY'RE OUT OF RANGE.
IT CAME FROM ONBOARD THE STATION.

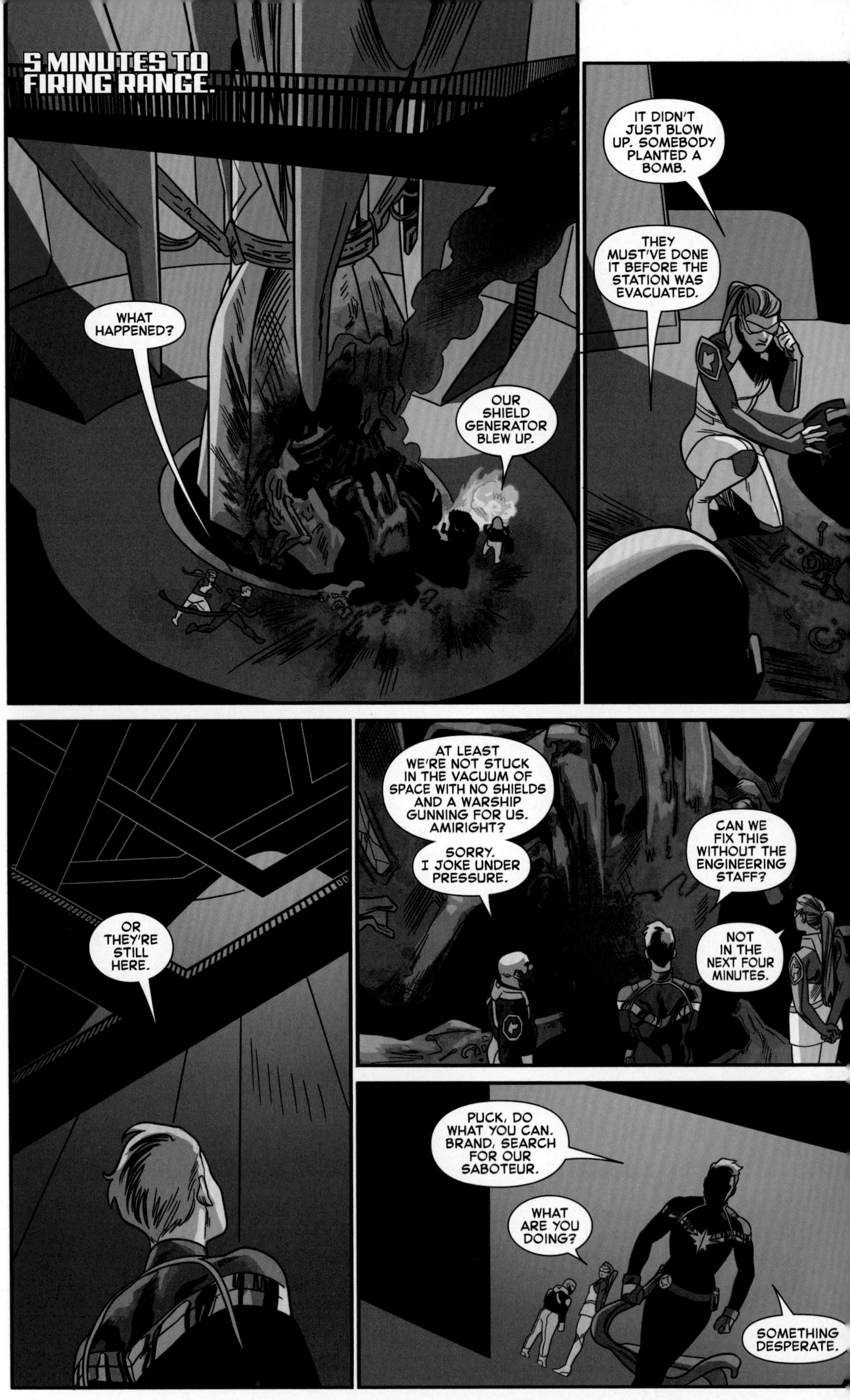
5 MINUTES TO FIRING RANGE.
WHAT HAPPENED?
OUR SHIELD GENERATOR BLEW UP.
IT DIDN'T JUST BLOW UP. SOMEBODY PLANTED A BOMB.
THEY MUST'VE DONE IT BEFORE THE STATION WAS EVACUATED.
OR THEY'RE STILL HERE.
AT LEAST WE'RE NOT STUCK IN THE VACUUM OF SPACE WITH NO SHIELDS AND A WARSHIP GUNNING FOR US. AMIRIGHT?
SORRY. I JOKE UNDER PRESSURE.
CAN WE FIX THIS WITHOUT THE ENGINEERING STAFF?
NOT IN THE NEXT FOUR MINUTES.
PUCK, DO WHAT YOU CAN. BRAND, SEARCH FOR OUR SABOTEUR.
WHAT ARE YOU DOING?
SOMETHING DESPERATE.

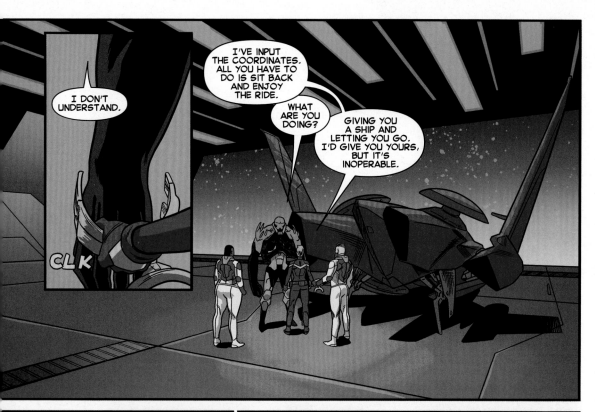

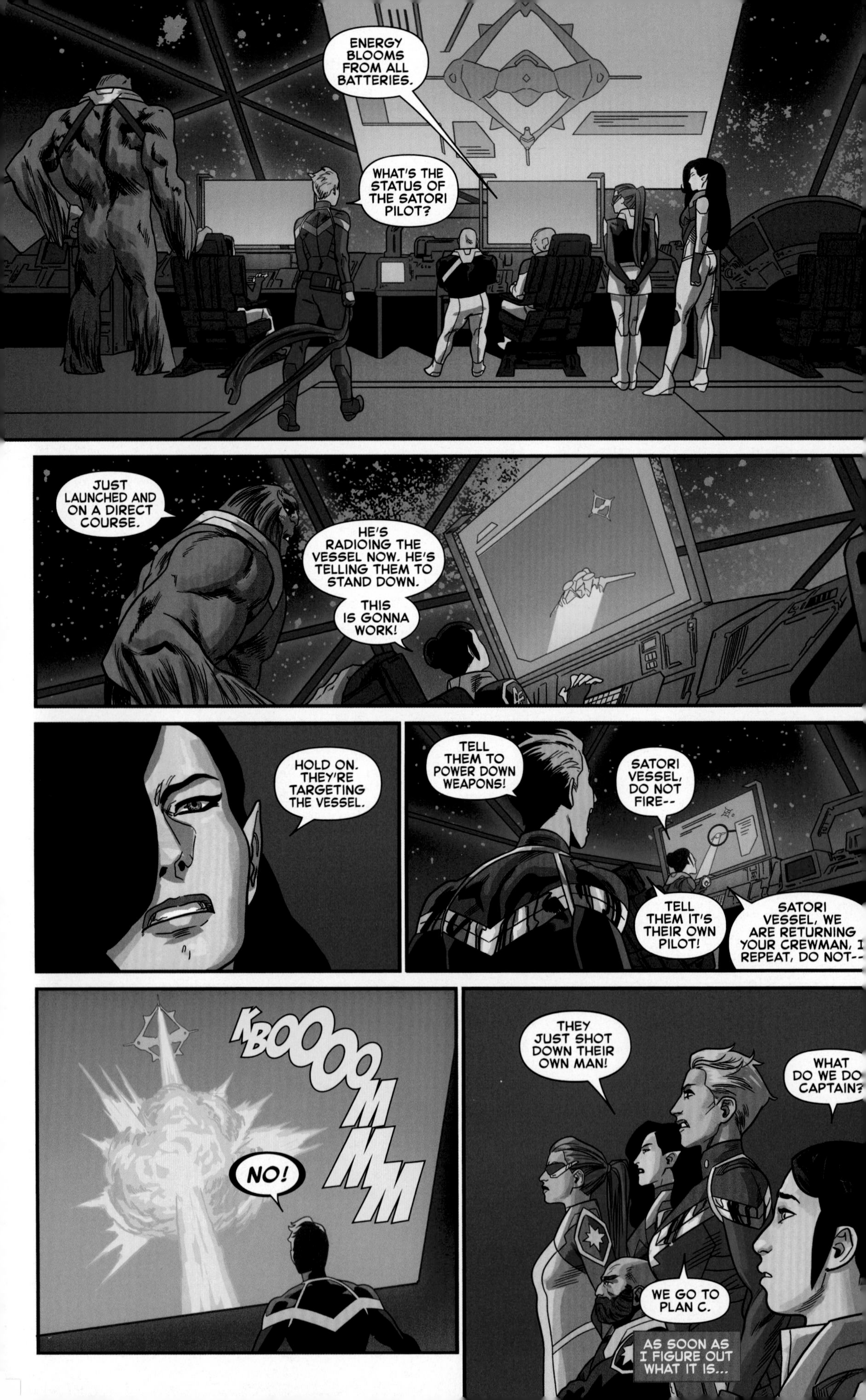
ENERGY BLOOMS FROM ALL BATTERIES.
WHAT'S THE STATUS OF THE SATORI PILOT?
JUST LAUNCHED AND ON A DIRECT COURSE.
HE'S RADIOING THE VESSEL NOW. HE'S TELLING THEM TO STAND DOWN.
THIS IS GONNA WORK!
HOLD ON. THEY'RE TARGETING THE VESSEL.
TELL THEM TO POWER DOWN WEAPONS!
SATORI VESSEL, DO NOT FIRE--
TELL THEM IT'S THEIR OWN PILOT!
SATORI VESSEL, WE ARE RETURNING YOUR CREWMAN, I REPEAT, DO NOT--
KBOOOOOMMMM
NO!
THEY JUST SHOT DOWN THEIR OWN MAN!
WHAT DO WE DO CAPTAIN?
WE GO TO PLAN C.
AS SOON AS I FIGURE OUT WHAT IT IS...

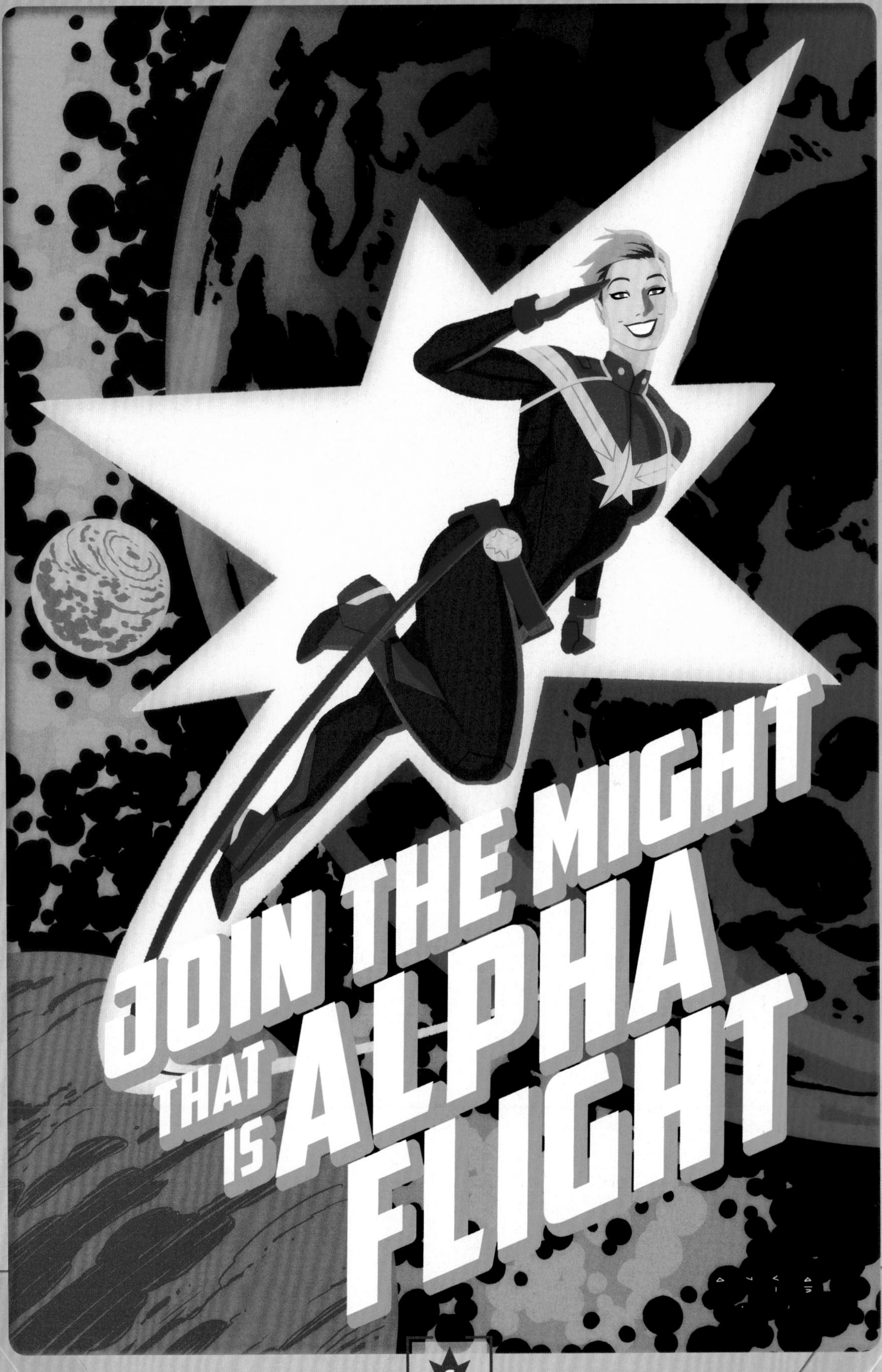
JOIN THE MIGHT THAT IS ALPHA FLIGHT

SHRAAM

SHIELDS ARE HOLDING.

GOOD WORK, PUCK AND WENDY.

AND BRYAN.

THIS ONLY BUYS US TIME, AND NOT A LOT. WE'RE NEVER GOING TO BEAT THEM WITH FIREPOWER.

BUT WE MAY BE ABLE TO USE THEIR OWN TECHNOLOGY AGAINST THEM.

THEIR SHIPS ARE LINKED--ALMOST LIKE ORGANISMS WITHIN AN ECOLOGICAL SYSTEM.

WE BELIEVE THAT IF WE AFFECT ONE ORGANISM, THE OTHER WILL BE EQUALLY AFFECTED.

FOR INSTANCE, WITH A VIRUS. SPECIFICALLY DESIGNED TO DISRUPT THE VESSEL'S SYSTEMS.

SOUNDS LIKE YOU'RE DESCRIBING A BIOLOGICAL WEAPON.

NO. IT AFFECTS THE SHIPS. NOT THE CREW. HOW QUICKLY CAN THIS HAPPEN?

IMMEDIATELY.

DO IT.

WARSHAUER AND I WILL HOLD DOWN THE FORT HERE.

AND WHAT AM I SUPPOSED TO BE DOING?

MAKING SURE WHOEVER TOOK OUT OUR SHIELDS DOESN'T DO IT AGAIN.

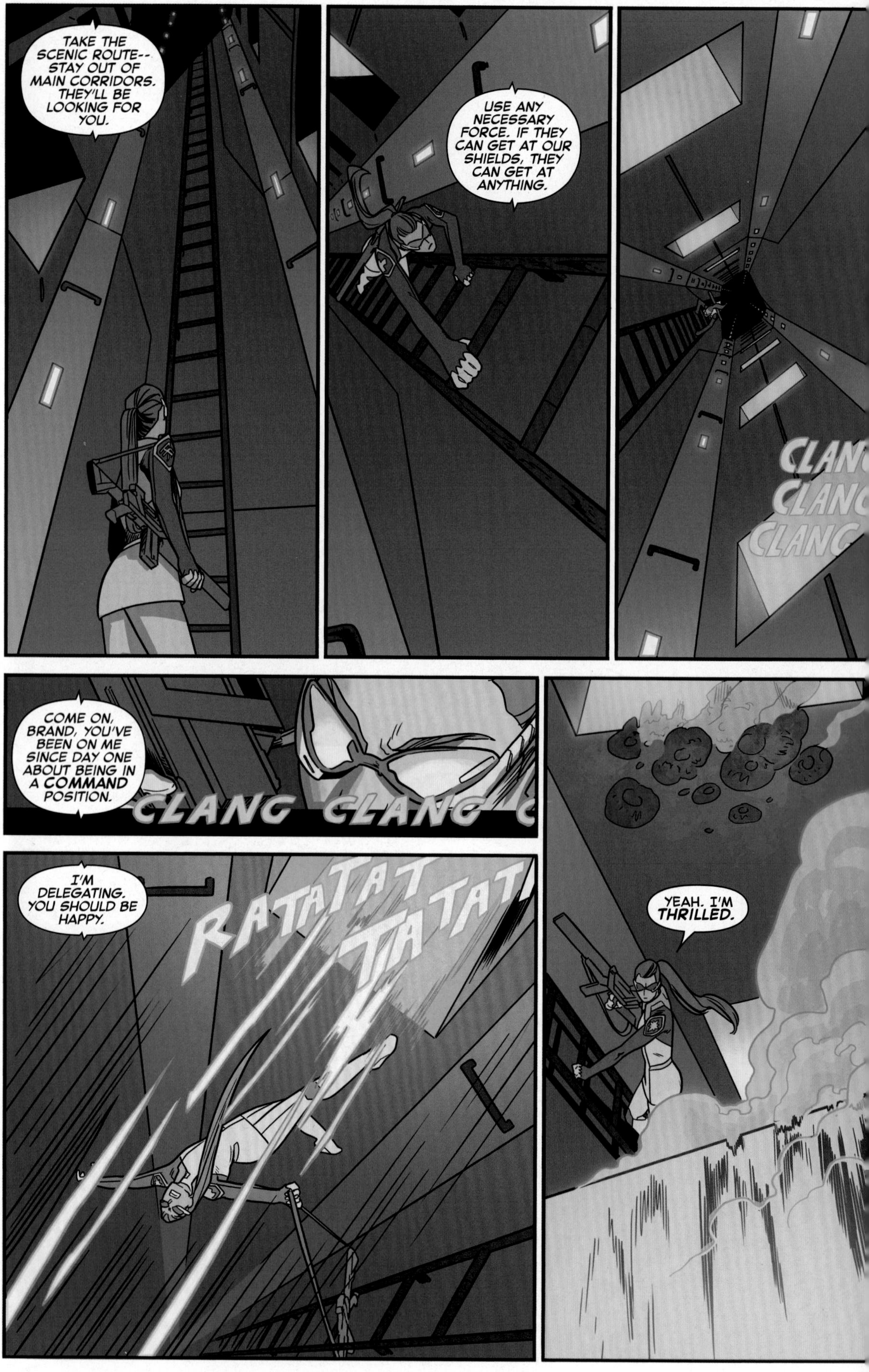
TAKE THE SCENIC ROUTE--STAY OUT OF MAIN CORRIDORS. THEY'LL BE LOOKING FOR YOU.
USE ANY NECESSARY FORCE. IF THEY CAN GET AT OUR SHIELDS, THEY CAN GET AT ANYTHING.
CLANG CLANG CLANG
COME ON, BRAND, YOU'VE BEEN ON ME SINCE DAY ONE ABOUT BEING IN A **COMMAND** POSITION.
CLANG CLANG
I'M DELEGATING. YOU SHOULD BE HAPPY.
RATATAT TATAT
YEAH. I'M **THRILLED.**

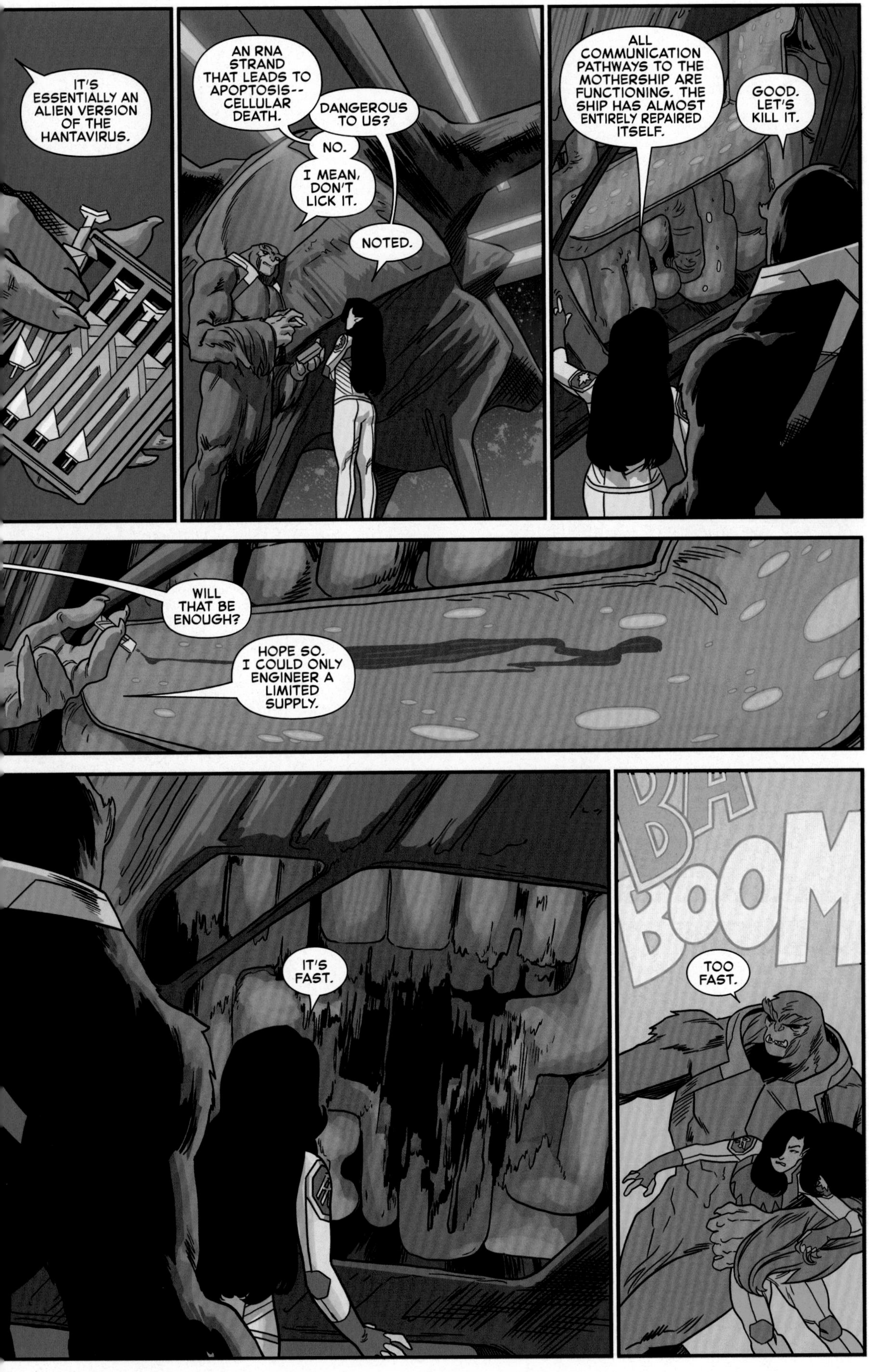
IT'S ESSENTIALLY AN ALIEN VERSION OF THE HANTAVIRUS.
AN RNA STRAND THAT LEADS TO APOPTOSIS-- CELLULAR DEATH.
DANGEROUS TO US?
NO.
I MEAN, DON'T LICK IT.
NOTED.
ALL COMMUNICATION PATHWAYS TO THE MOTHERSHIP ARE FUNCTIONING. THE SHIP HAS ALMOST ENTIRELY REPAIRED ITSELF.
GOOD. LET'S KILL IT.
WILL THAT BE ENOUGH?
HOPE SO. I COULD ONLY ENGINEER A LIMITED SUPPLY.
IT'S FAST.
BA BOOM
TOO FAST.

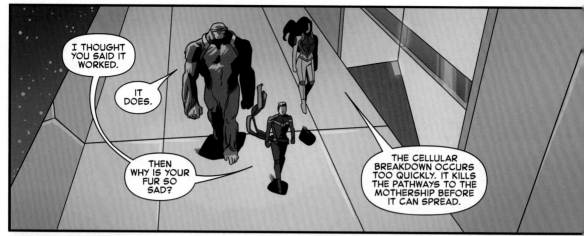

I THOUGHT YOU SAID IT WORKED.

IT DOES.

THEN WHY IS YOUR FUR SO SAD?

THE CELLULAR BREAKDOWN OCCURS TOO QUICKLY. IT KILLS THE PATHWAYS TO THE MOTHERSHIP BEFORE IT CAN SPREAD.

CAN YOU FIX IT?

IN TWELVE HOURS.

BOOM

WE DON'T HAVE TWELVE *MINUTES* AT THIS RATE. I NEED OTHER OPTIONS.

WE'D HAVE TO FIND A WAY TO DIRECTLY DELIVER THE VIRUS TO THE MOTHERSHIP.

CAN WE ARM A MISSILE?

THE EXPLOSION WOULD DESTROY THE VIRUS.

THEN THERE'S ONLY ONE THING TO DO.

OPEN A LINE TO THE SATORI VESSEL.

THEY HAVEN'T BEEN RESPONDING TO--

THEY'LL RESPOND TO THIS.

Dbrruumbbll

THAT WAS A BIG ONE. OUR SHIELDS DROPPED BACK TO FIFTY PERCENT--

THE CHANNEL IS OPEN TO THE SATORI VESSEL, CAPTAIN.

SATORI VESSEL. THIS IS...

...THIS IS *MAR-VELL*. OF THE KREE IMPERIAL MILITIA.

WHAT DID SHE SAY?

DANVERS, WHAT THE HELL ARE YOU *DOING*?

IF YOU CEASE FIRE IMMEDIATELY AND LEAVE THIS SYSTEM...

I WILL SURRENDER MYSELF TO YOUR CUSTODY.

NO--!

SHUT DOWN THE LINK! SHUT IT DOWN NOW!

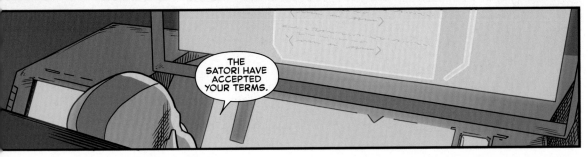

THE SATORI HAVE ACCEPTED YOUR TERMS.

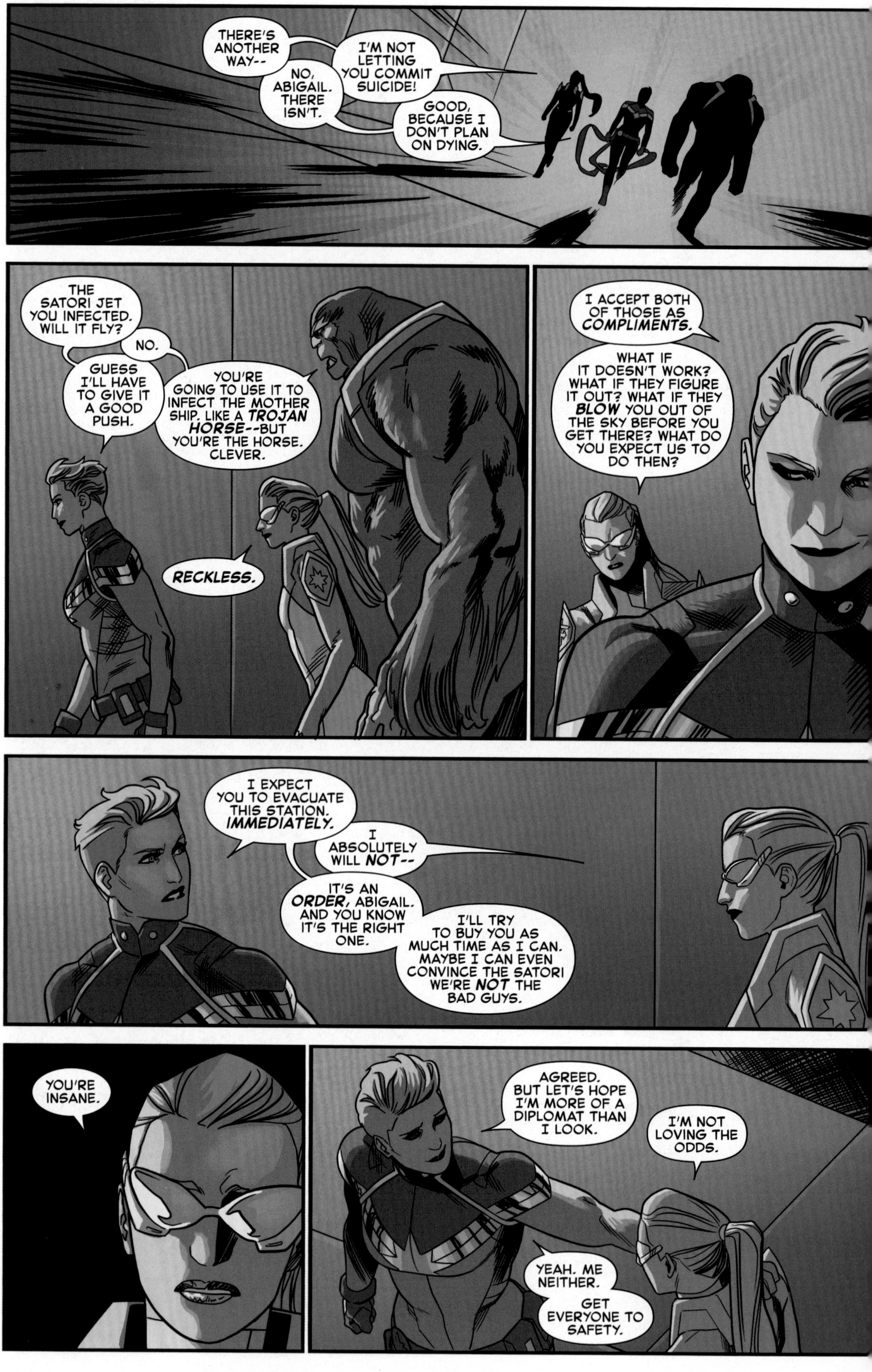
THERE'S ANOTHER WAY--
I'M NOT LETTING YOU COMMIT SUICIDE!
NO, ABIGAIL. THERE ISN'T.
GOOD, BECAUSE I DON'T PLAN ON DYING.
THE SATORI JET YOU INFECTED. WILL IT FLY?
NO.
GUESS I'LL HAVE TO GIVE IT A GOOD PUSH.
YOU'RE GOING TO USE IT TO INFECT THE MOTHER SHIP. LIKE A TROJAN HORSE--BUT YOU'RE THE HORSE. CLEVER.
RECKLESS.
I ACCEPT BOTH OF THOSE AS COMPLIMENTS.
WHAT IF IT DOESN'T WORK? WHAT IF THEY FIGURE IT OUT? WHAT IF THEY BLOW YOU OUT OF THE SKY BEFORE YOU GET THERE? WHAT DO YOU EXPECT US TO DO THEN?
I EXPECT YOU TO EVACUATE THIS STATION. IMMEDIATELY.
I ABSOLUTELY WILL NOT--
IT'S AN ORDER, ABIGAIL. AND YOU KNOW IT'S THE RIGHT ONE.
I'LL TRY TO BUY YOU AS MUCH TIME AS I CAN. MAYBE I CAN EVEN CONVINCE THE SATORI WE'RE NOT THE BAD GUYS.
YOU'RE INSANE.
AGREED. BUT LET'S HOPE I'M MORE OF A DIPLOMAT THAN I LOOK.
I'M NOT LOVING THE ODDS.
YEAH. ME NEITHER.
GET EVERYONE TO SAFETY.

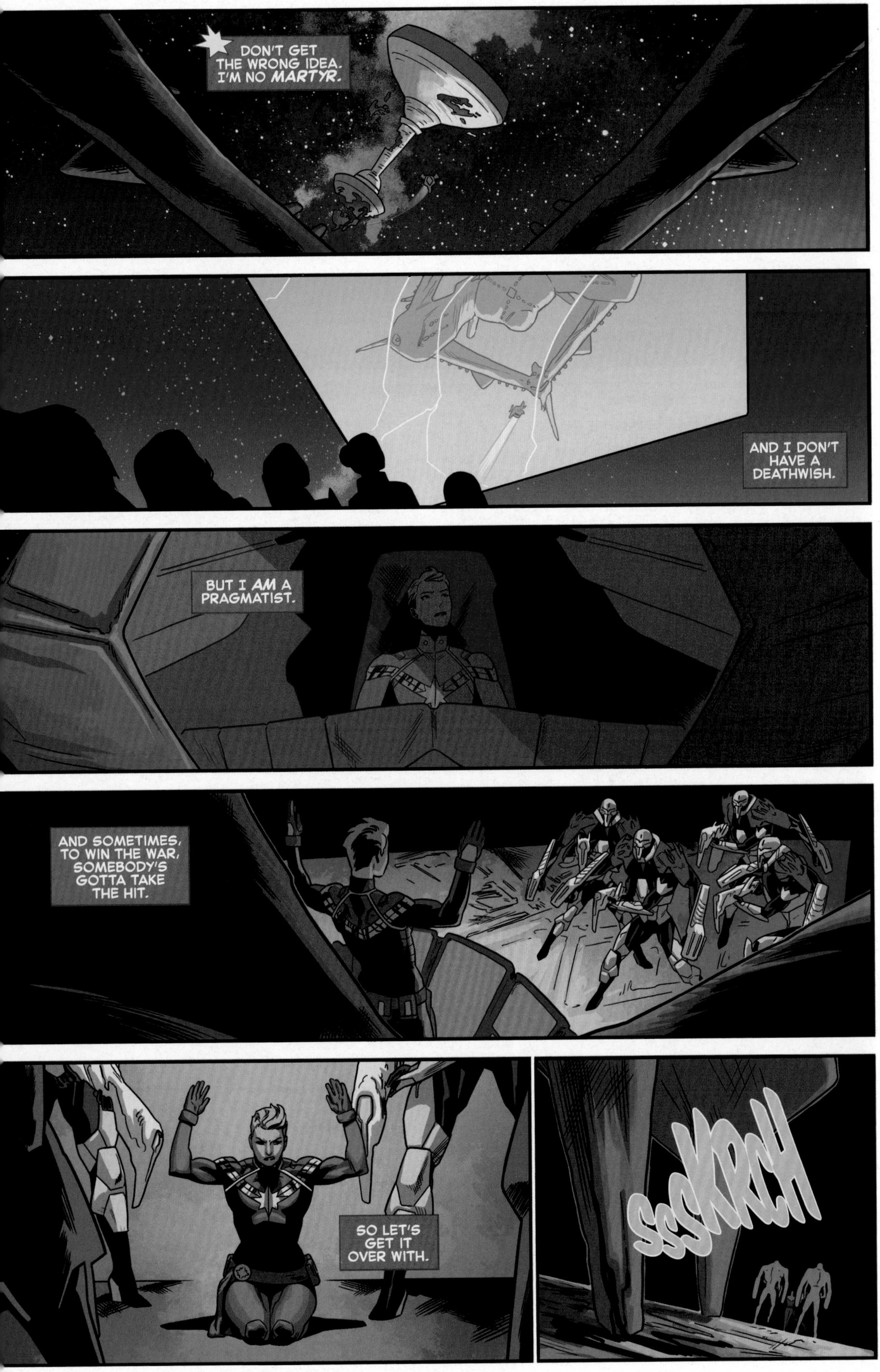
DON'T GET THE WRONG IDEA. I'M NO MARTYR.
AND I DON'T HAVE A DEATHWISH.
BUT I AM A PRAGMATIST.
AND SOMETIMES, TO WIN THE WAR, SOMEBODY'S GOTTA TAKE THE HIT.
SO LET'S GET IT OVER WITH.
SSSKRCH

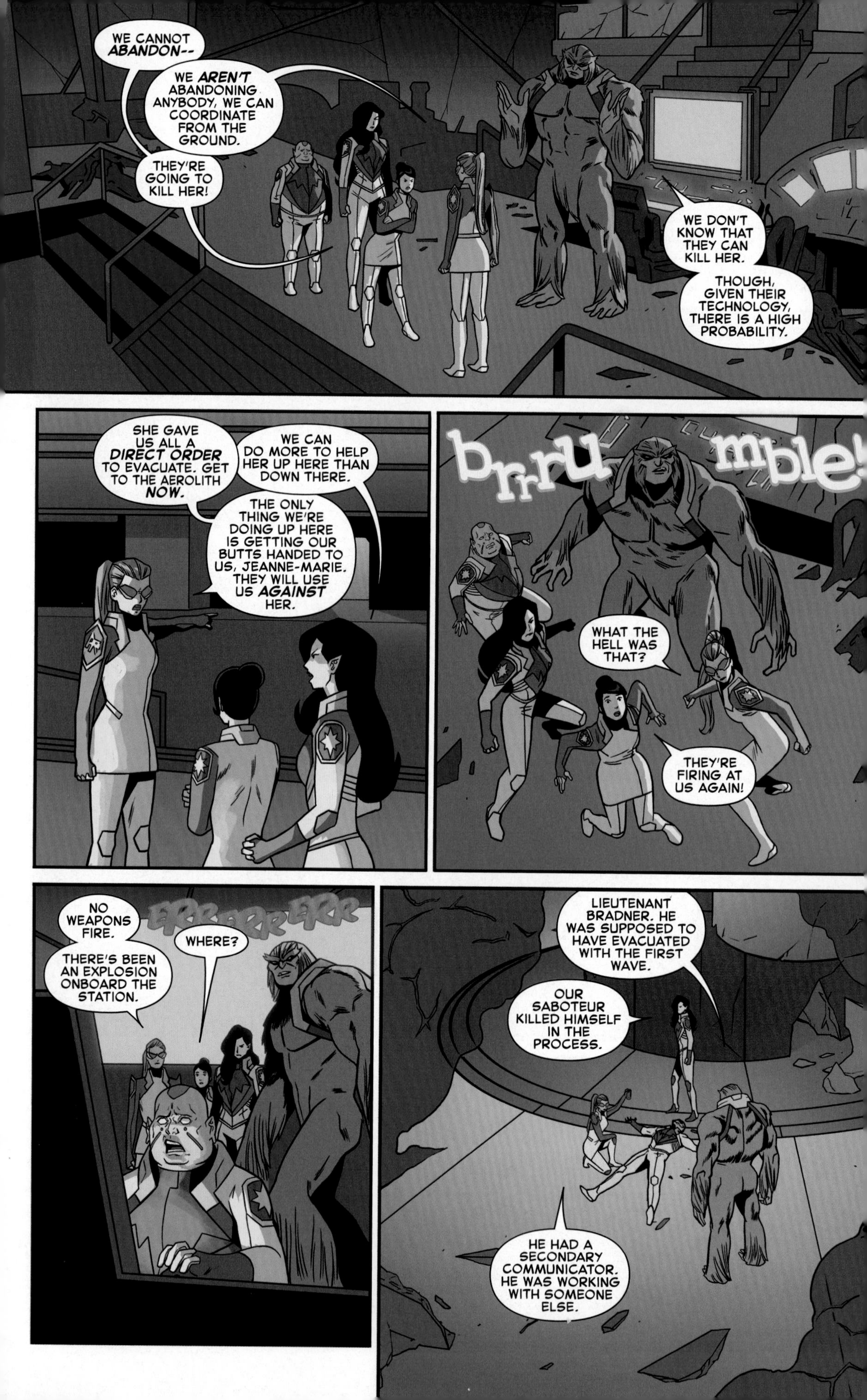
WE CANNOT ABANDON--
WE AREN'T ABANDONING ANYBODY, WE CAN COORDINATE FROM THE GROUND.
THEY'RE GOING TO KILL HER!
WE DON'T KNOW THAT THEY CAN KILL HER.
THOUGH, GIVEN THEIR TECHNOLOGY, THERE IS A HIGH PROBABILITY.
SHE GAVE US ALL A DIRECT ORDER TO EVACUATE. GET TO THE AEROLITH NOW.
WE CAN DO MORE TO HELP HER UP HERE THAN DOWN THERE.
THE ONLY THING WE'RE DOING UP HERE IS GETTING OUR BUTTS HANDED TO US, JEANNE-MARIE. THEY WILL USE US AGAINST HER.
brrrumble!
WHAT THE HELL WAS THAT?
THEY'RE FIRING AT US AGAIN!
ERRRERRRERR
NO WEAPONS FIRE.
THERE'S BEEN AN EXPLOSION ONBOARD THE STATION.
WHERE?
LIEUTENANT BRADNER. HE WAS SUPPOSED TO HAVE EVACUATED WITH THE FIRST WAVE.
OUR SABOTEUR KILLED HIMSELF IN THE PROCESS.
HE HAD A SECONDARY COMMUNICATOR. HE WAS WORKING WITH SOMEONE ELSE.

IT'S A TRANSLATOR. IF I REALLY WANTED TO KILL YOU, WHY WOULD WE BE TRYING TO UNDERSTAND YOU?

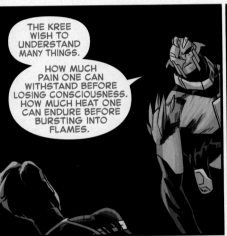

THE KREE WISH TO UNDERSTAND MANY THINGS.

HOW MUCH PAIN ONE CAN WITHSTAND BEFORE LOSING CONSCIOUSNESS. HOW MUCH HEAT ONE CAN ENDURE BEFORE BURSTING INTO FLAMES.

THAT ISN'T ME.

YOU ARE GENETICALLY KREE!

I WAS BORN HUMAN. AND IF YOU'VE GOT AN HOUR I CAN TRY AND EXPLAIN HOW THE HELL THAT HAPPENED.

AND YET YOU WEAR THE HALA STAR.

WELL... THAT SEEMED LIKE A GOOD IDEA AT THE TIME.

THE KREE DESTROYED OUR HOMEWORLD!

AND NOW THE THE KREE HOMEWORLD HAS BEEN DESTROYED. YOU'RE FIGHTING A WAR THAT'S ALREADY OVER.

MAR-VELL OF KREE CAME TO THIS PLANET AND FOUGHT FOR JUSTICE. HE CHANGED. I BELIEVE YOU CAN DO THE SAME.

THIS IS JUSTICE, MAR-VELL.

UNH!

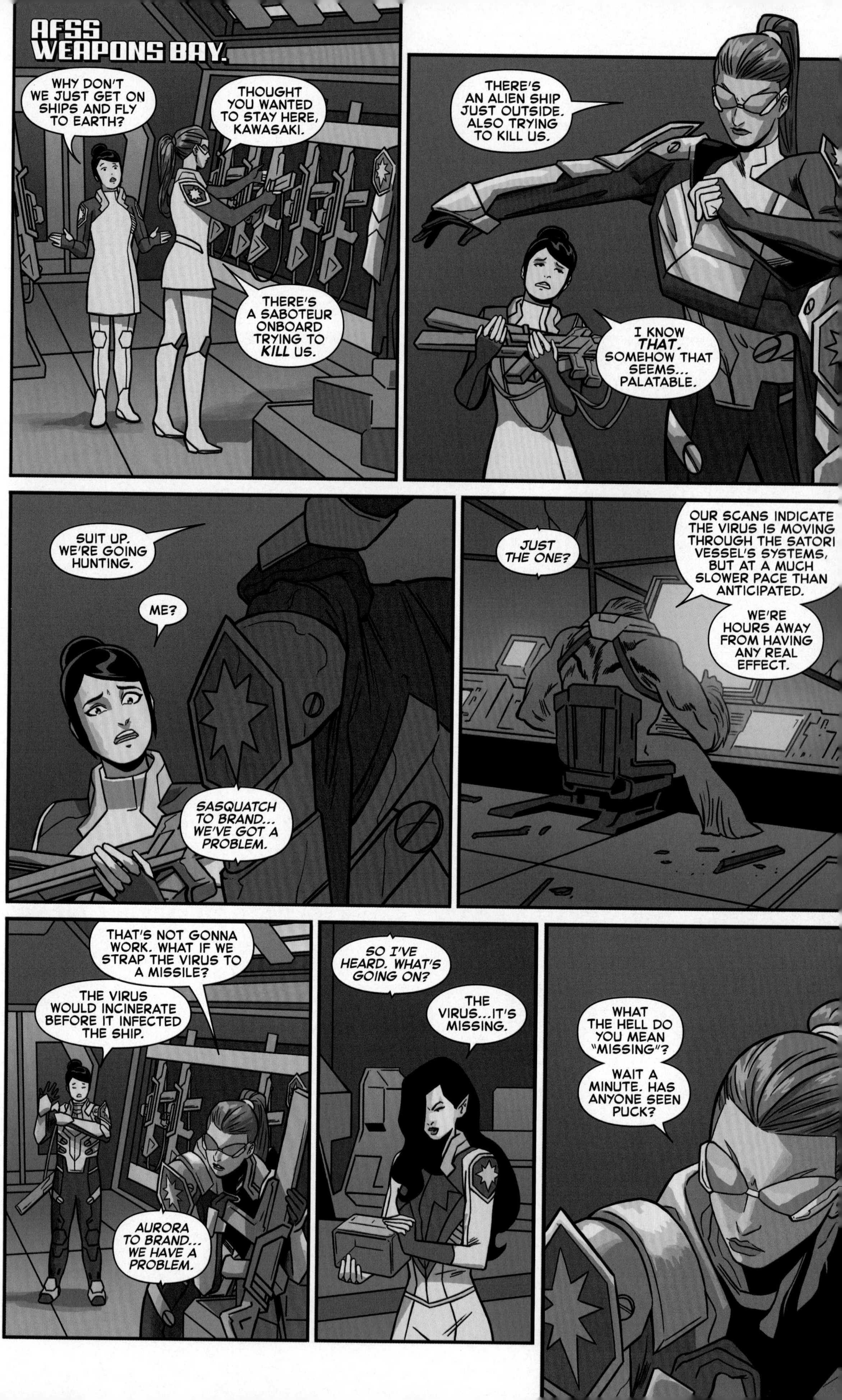
AFSS WEAPONS BAY.
WHY DON'T WE JUST GET ON SHIPS AND FLY TO EARTH?
THOUGHT YOU WANTED TO STAY HERE, KAWASAKI.
THERE'S A SABOTEUR ONBOARD TRYING TO *KILL* US.
THERE'S AN ALIEN SHIP JUST OUTSIDE. ALSO TRYING TO KILL US.
I KNOW *THAT.* SOMEHOW THAT SEEMS... PALATABLE.
SUIT UP. WE'RE GOING HUNTING.
ME?
SASQUATCH TO BRAND... WE'VE GOT A PROBLEM.
JUST THE ONE?
OUR SCANS INDICATE THE VIRUS IS MOVING THROUGH THE SATORI VESSEL'S SYSTEMS, BUT AT A MUCH SLOWER PACE THAN ANTICIPATED.
WE'RE HOURS AWAY FROM HAVING ANY REAL EFFECT.
THAT'S NOT GONNA WORK. WHAT IF WE STRAP THE VIRUS TO A MISSILE?
THE VIRUS WOULD INCINERATE BEFORE IT INFECTED THE SHIP.
AURORA TO BRAND... WE HAVE A PROBLEM.
SO I'VE HEARD. WHAT'S GOING ON?
THE VIRUS...IT'S MISSING.
WHAT THE HELL DO YOU MEAN "MISSING"?
WAIT A MINUTE. HAS ANYONE SEEN PUCK?

chunk

C'MON, CAROL.

IT'S THE LACK OF TRUST THAT REALLY TICKS ME OFF.

LIKE ALPHA FLIGHT IS SO INCOMPETENT THAT YOUR ONLY CHOICE IS TO SACRIFICE *YOURSELF* TO SAVE *US?*

THAT HURTS ME. THAT HURTS ME A LOT.

AND WHEN I'M HURT, I WILL SOMETIMES MAKE DECISIONS THAT COULD BE DEEMED RASH.

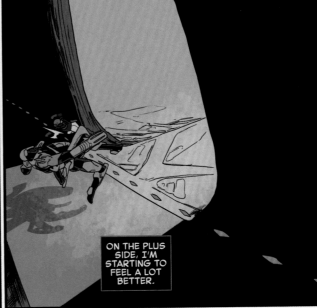

ON THE PLUS SIDE, I'M STARTING TO FEEL A LOT BETTER.

DELETING SELECTED FILES REQUIRES PASSWORD
*****_

DON'T DO IT, GARCIA.

IT PROBABLY GOES WITHOUT SAYING, BUT YOU ARE VERY FIRED.

FOR DOING MY DUTY? FOR PROTECTING THE EARTH?

HOW 'BOUT FOR BEING A *TRAITOR?*

HEH, YOU'LL HAVE TO PROVE IT FIRST.

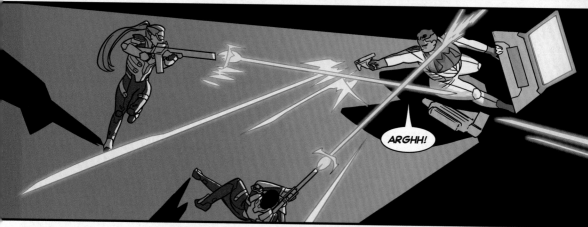

ARGHH!

WHERE'D YOU LEARN TO SHOOT LIKE THAT, KAWASAKI?

UM... MOSTLY LASER TAG.

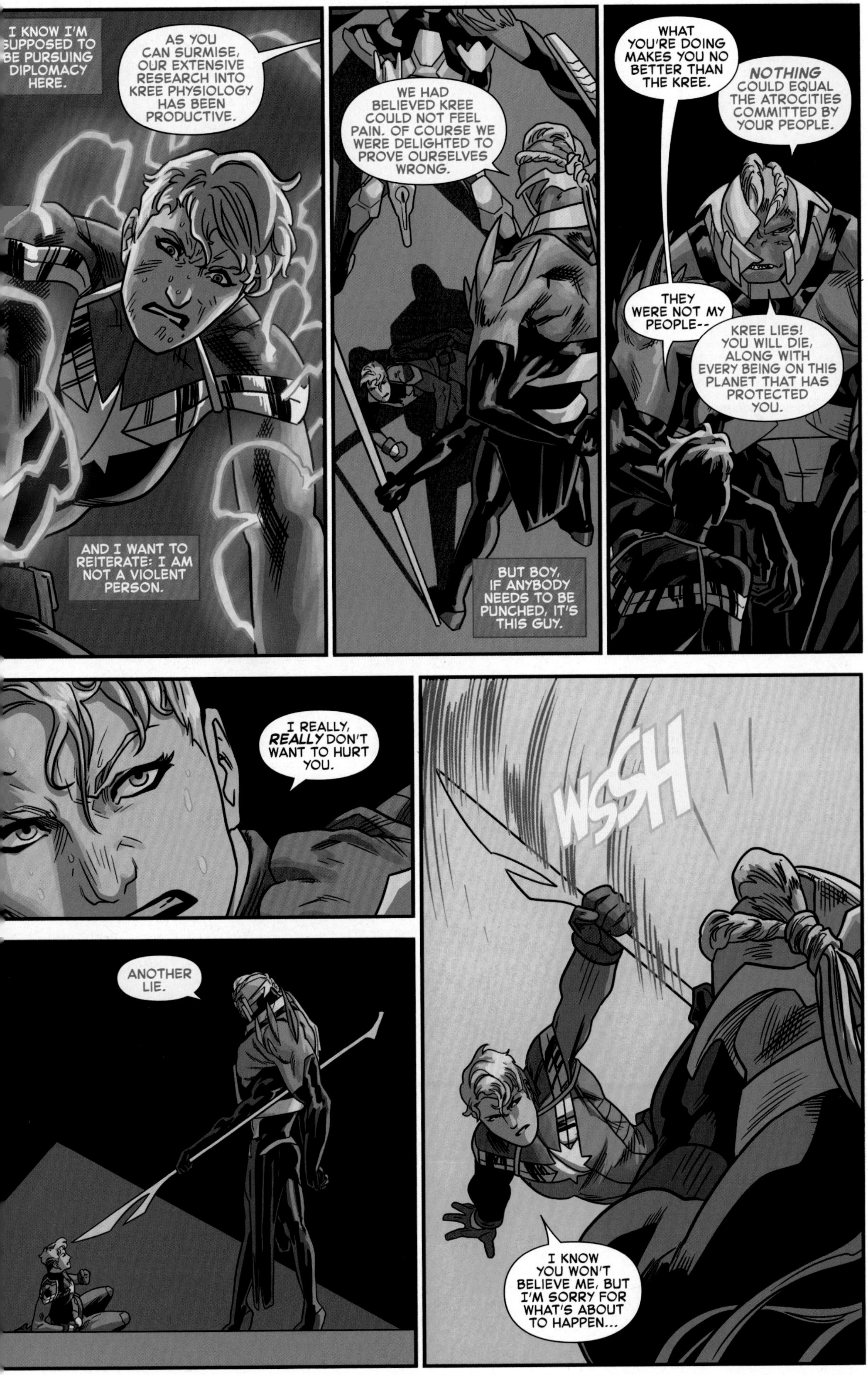
I KNOW I'M SUPPOSED TO BE PURSUING DIPLOMACY HERE.
AS YOU CAN SURMISE, OUR EXTENSIVE RESEARCH INTO KREE PHYSIOLOGY HAS BEEN PRODUCTIVE.
AND I WANT TO REITERATE: I AM NOT A VIOLENT PERSON.
WE HAD BELIEVED KREE COULD NOT FEEL PAIN. OF COURSE WE WERE DELIGHTED TO PROVE OURSELVES WRONG.
BUT BOY, IF ANYBODY NEEDS TO BE PUNCHED, IT'S THIS GUY.
WHAT YOU'RE DOING MAKES YOU NO BETTER THAN THE KREE.
NOTHING COULD EQUAL THE ATROCITIES COMMITTED BY YOUR PEOPLE.
THEY WERE NOT MY PEOPLE--
KREE LIES! YOU WILL DIE, ALONG WITH EVERY BEING ON THIS PLANET THAT HAS PROTECTED YOU.
I REALLY, *REALLY* DON'T WANT TO HURT YOU.
ANOTHER LIE.
WSSH
I KNOW YOU WON'T BELIEVE ME, BUT I'M SORRY FOR WHAT'S ABOUT TO HAPPEN...

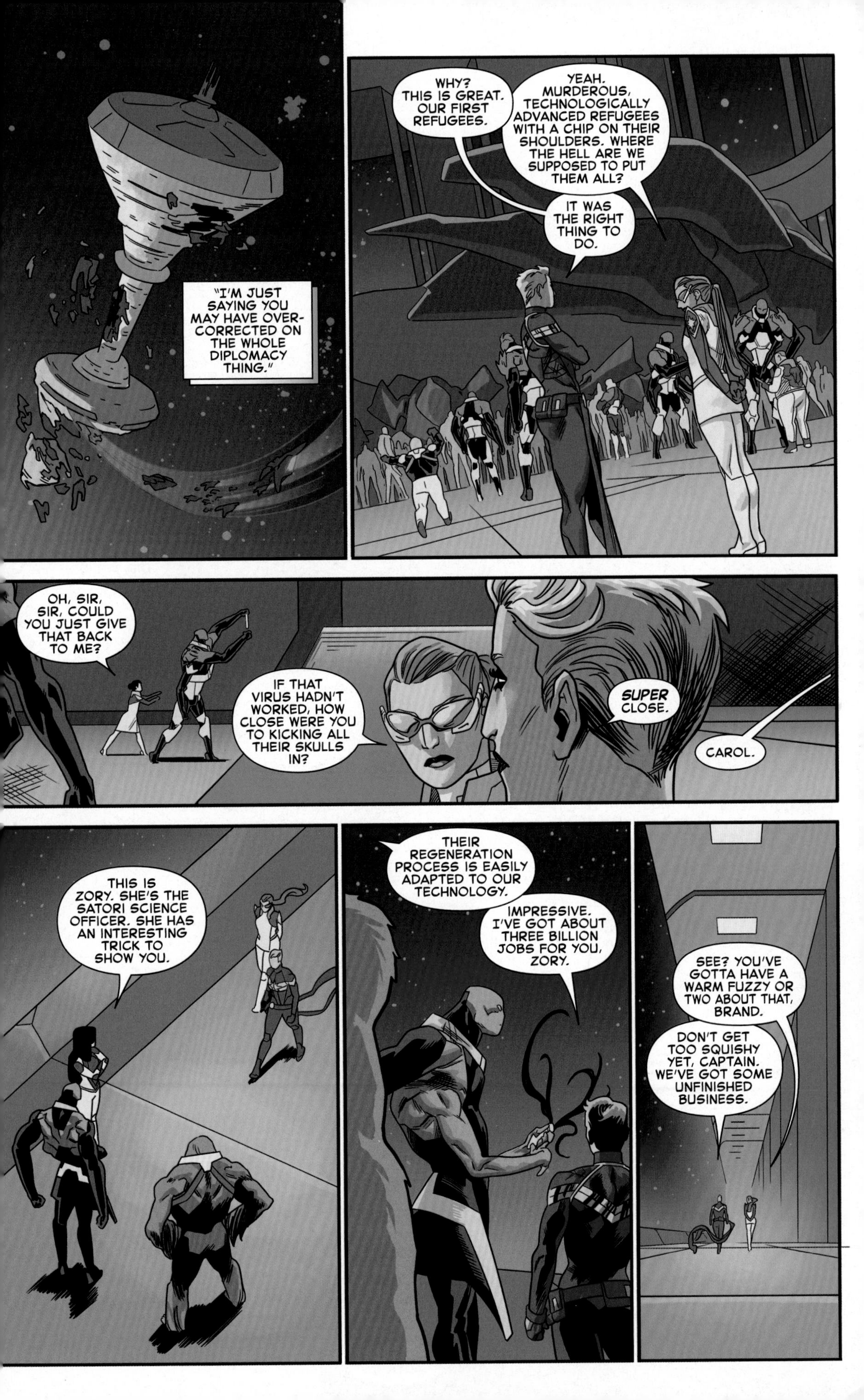
"I'M JUST SAYING YOU MAY HAVE OVER-CORRECTED ON THE WHOLE DIPLOMACY THING."
WHY? THIS IS GREAT. OUR FIRST REFUGEES.
YEAH. MURDEROUS, TECHNOLOGICALLY ADVANCED REFUGEES WITH A CHIP ON THEIR SHOULDERS. WHERE THE HELL ARE WE SUPPOSED TO PUT THEM ALL?
IT WAS THE RIGHT THING TO DO.
OH, SIR, SIR, COULD YOU JUST GIVE THAT BACK TO ME?
IF THAT VIRUS HADN'T WORKED, HOW CLOSE WERE YOU TO KICKING ALL THEIR SKULLS IN?
SUPER CLOSE.
CAROL.
THIS IS ZORY. SHE'S THE SATORI SCIENCE OFFICER. SHE HAS AN INTERESTING TRICK TO SHOW YOU.
THEIR REGENERATION PROCESS IS EASILY ADAPTED TO OUR TECHNOLOGY.
IMPRESSIVE. I'VE GOT ABOUT THREE BILLION JOBS FOR YOU, ZORY.
SEE? YOU'VE GOTTA HAVE A WARM FUZZY OR TWO ABOUT THAT, BRAND.
DON'T GET TOO SQUISHY YET, CAPTAIN. WE'VE GOT SOME UNFINISHED BUSINESS.

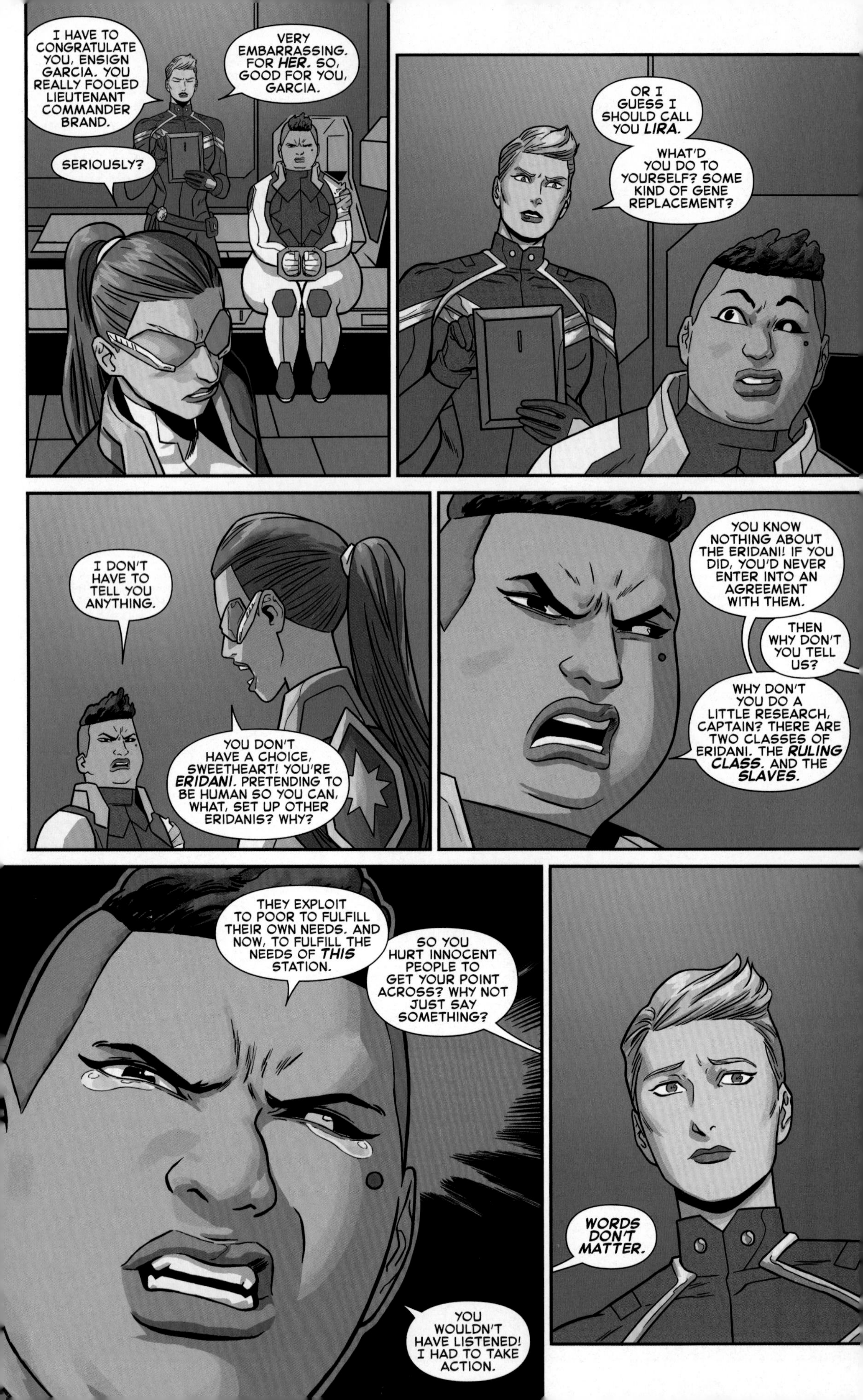
I HAVE TO CONGRATULATE YOU, ENSIGN GARCIA. YOU REALLY FOOLED LIEUTENANT COMMANDER BRAND.
VERY EMBARRASSING. FOR *HER.* SO, GOOD FOR YOU, GARCIA.
SERIOUSLY?
OR I GUESS I SHOULD CALL YOU *LIRA.*
WHAT'D YOU DO TO YOURSELF? SOME KIND OF GENE REPLACEMENT?
I DON'T HAVE TO TELL YOU ANYTHING.
YOU DON'T HAVE A CHOICE, SWEETHEART! YOU'RE *ERIDANI.* PRETENDING TO BE HUMAN SO YOU CAN, WHAT, SET UP OTHER ERIDANIS? WHY?
YOU KNOW NOTHING ABOUT THE ERIDANI! IF YOU DID, YOU'D NEVER ENTER INTO AN AGREEMENT WITH THEM.
THEN WHY DON'T YOU TELL US?
WHY DON'T YOU DO A LITTLE RESEARCH, CAPTAIN? THERE ARE TWO CLASSES OF ERIDANI. THE *RULING CLASS.* AND THE *SLAVES.*
THEY EXPLOIT TO POOR TO FULFILL THEIR OWN NEEDS. AND NOW, TO FULFILL THE NEEDS OF *THIS* STATION.
SO YOU HURT INNOCENT PEOPLE TO GET YOUR POINT ACROSS? WHY NOT JUST SAY SOMETHING?
YOU WOULDN'T HAVE LISTENED! I HAD TO TAKE ACTION.
WORDS DON'T MATTER.

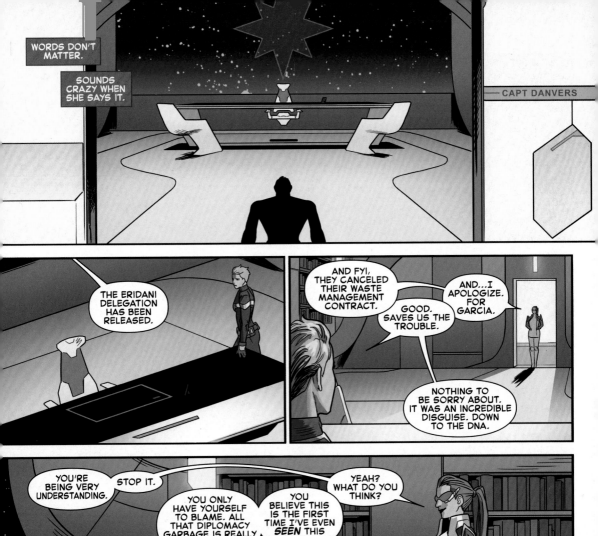

#2 VARIANT BY PHIL JIMENEZ & MARTE GRACIA

captain
MARVEL

#2 VARIANT BY MICHAEL CHO

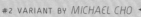

#3 VARIANT BY
JAMIE McKELVIE & MATTHEW WILSON

#3 WOMEN OF POWER VARIANT BY
EMANUELA LUPACCHINO & GURU-eFX

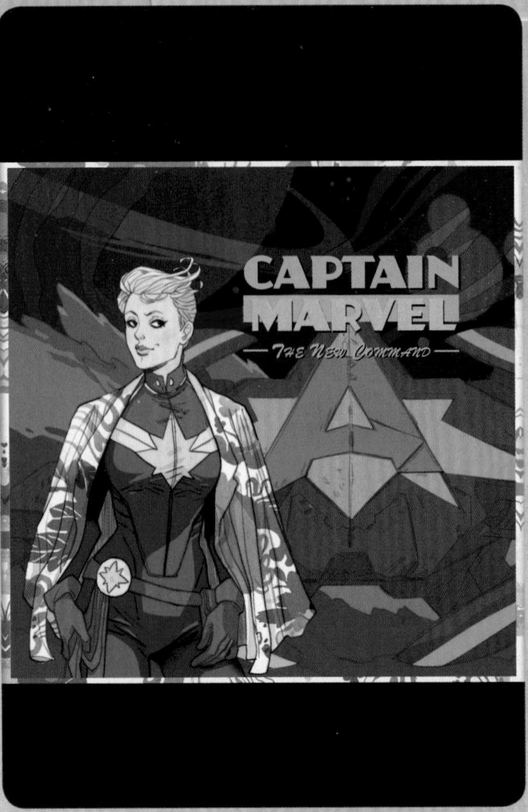
CAPTAIN
MARVEL
THE NEW COMMAND

#1 HIP-HOP VARIANT BY *MARGUERITE SAUVAGE*

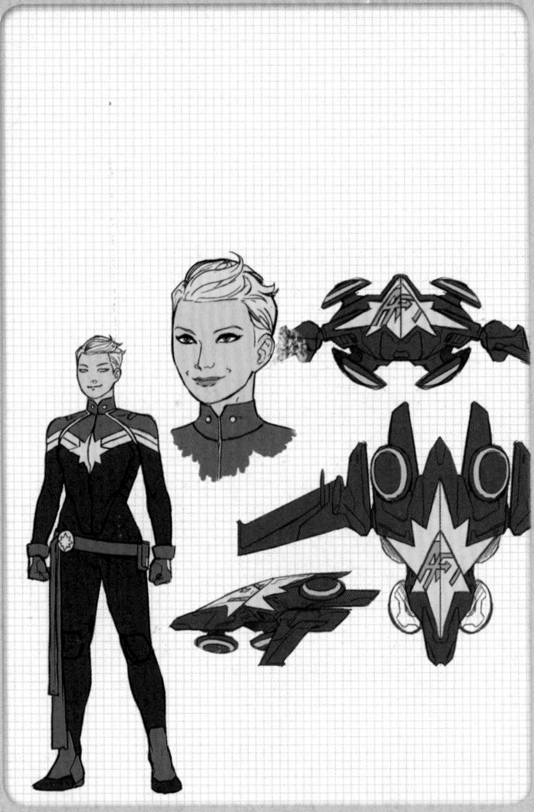

#1 DESIGN VARIANT BY *KRIS ANKA*

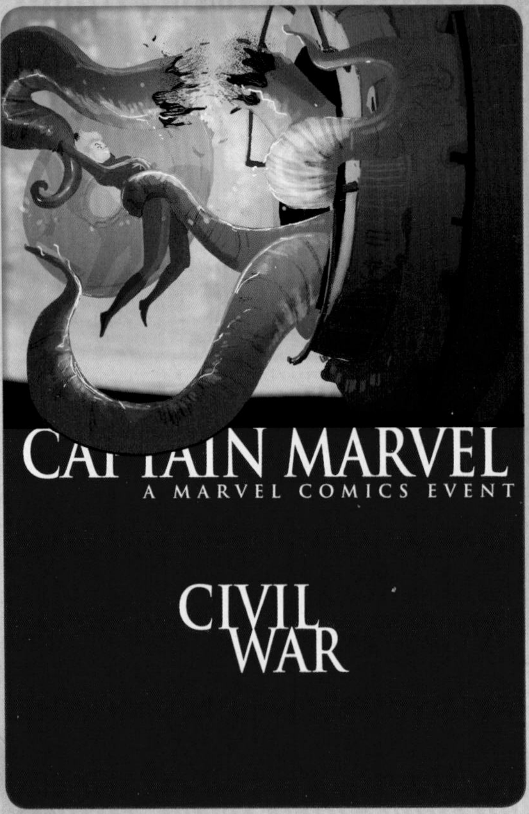
CAPTAIN MARVEL
A MARVEL COMICS EVENT
CIVIL
WAR

#4 CIVIL WAR VARIANT BY *PASCAL CAMPION*

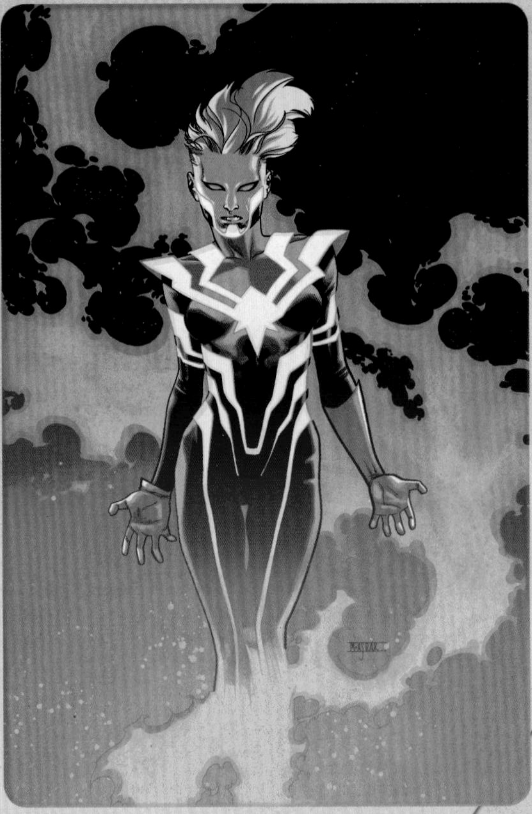

#5 AGE OF APOCALYPSE VARIANT BY *MAHMUD ASRAR & DAVE McCAIG*